T0187059

SeniorITy

How AI and tech can
enhance senior living

LUCIA DORE &
CAROLE RAILTON

First published in Great Britain in 2023 by

a R⍨think Press company

Panoma Press Ltd
www.rethinkpress.com
www.panomapress.com

Cover design and book layout by Neil Coe
Cover Robotic Hand image by rawpixel.com on Freepik
Cover Trainline image by tawatchai07 on Freepik
Other cover images: Freepik.com

978-1-784529-68-0

Lucia would like to dedicate this book to her late father, who died in his mid-eighties. He was its inspiration; although he liked technology, he wanted to be better at using it. Lucia spent hours showing him how to navigate the internet and make the most of his cell phone.

Carole would like to dedicate this book to anyone struggling with learning new technology so that they can feel included rather than on the edge. Carole has found technology to be of great benefit to her and she hopes others will find it as useful.

Contents

Introduction

When human beings look back on this time in history, we will notice that we were part of a behavioral shift. Much of this shift involves technology and artificial intelligence (AI) in particular. This book will look at how seniors have to deal with this shift, keep up with new developments and make the most of them. It will give them the information they need to have more progressive and cohesive lives and take part in the future.

It's critical for seniors to feel comfortable interacting with technology, especially those in their later years. Many are already using AI, but they need support systems around them to take advantage of their experience and learn how new technology can make life in their senior years better. In this book, we will look at every aspect of life with technology, the benefits and the pitfalls. We'll examine how to manage the latest developments, including social media, and point out the most likely future to expect. We (the authors) have undertaken plenty of research with a range of people, including criminologists, futurists, designers, high-tech developers and trainers of seniors, as well as citing a host of books and articles to create the content of this book.

Time seems to move ever more quickly as one gets older, so it makes sense to enhance your experiences and have the best possible outcomes in later life. When you're aware of roughly how much time you have left, knowing how new technology, including AI, can ease your life and give you better experiences is invaluable. Understanding what is going on in the world and how to manage it gives you the power to control and develop your everyday life. This book will make sure you get the best of both worlds: the high-tech and the personal experiences.

Older people are all part of the future, so this book will draw on the knowledge of those at the forefront of technology and show how this can benefit society as a whole and seniors in particular. It will tackle common concerns as well as showing how to deal with technology going forward. Without this information, you are likely to fall behind and may find yourself needing the help of other people to navigate the world.

For the purpose of this book, deciding on what determines a "senior" has been difficult. Our working definition of "seniors" is anyone aged sixty or over, even though many people in their sixties and beyond do not feel old enough to be defined in this way. Some people who are younger than this, perhaps in their fifties, may find the advice in the pages of this book relevant to them too. Overall, people are living longer than they used to, often into their late eighties and nineties. Seventy has become the new fifty, so the concept of a senior is ever evolving. Whether you are considered old is based not only on how you define yourself, but also on how society perceives you. This is another area this book will discuss.

To illustrate the fact that the definition of a senior is an evolving one, we need look no further than a person's eligibility for the state pension in their country. Not only do people become eligible for the state pension at different ages in different countries, but the age of eligibility changes regularly within each country.

For example, in the United Kingdom, the age at which the state pension pays out is currently sixty-six, but it is due to rise to sixty-eight by 2028.[1] In New Zealand, sixty-five is the age at which you can receive the state pension;[2] in the United States, you can claim the full benefit at sixty-six years and two months if you were born no later than the 1950s, but this will rise to sixty-seven for those born in 1960 and beyond.[3] The increase in life expectancy is cited as one of the main reasons for the pensionable age increasing. Throw into the mix the fact that people don't have to stop working when they reach their pension age, and you get the general idea of how difficult it has been to define a senior.

We as the authors of this book are, in fact, seniors ourselves: Lucia Dore is sixty; Carole Railton is seventy-one. Working together we could combine our two skill sets – technology and the media. Because of our backgrounds we are well placed to know how seniors are making decisions regarding technology and AI, what they think about these disciplines and how they interact with technology.

We decided to write this book as we have a shared interest in what happens to seniors and have set up a business and created podcasts for a couple of years on this subject. We feel that the reluctance of seniors to use technology needs more attention and that they would benefit from greater awareness to maximize the benefits of technology. Moreover, we could see the people around us—our parents, our relatives, our friends and sometimes ourselves—were frustrated with all the necessary technology for modern living and we believed a book on the subject was one of the best ways to address this issue with seniors.

It's sad to say in this age of inclusivity, but those identified as seniors are often discriminated against simply because they are older. Seniors bring to the labor market a lot of experience and skills, which should be appreciated and seized upon, but employers sometimes assume that an older person won't be familiar with or able to operate the latest technology. They may even perceive seniors as not being at all au fait with technology, which can make finding a job tough when you reach a certain age. This is one reason why seniors may choose to become entrepreneurs instead of remaining in employment, but of course, that too will involve the use of technology.

A large number of older adults are accessing the internet and social media—sometimes, it has to be said, reluctantly—and many have used computers (albeit less sophisticated ones than are available now) during their careers. Despite this, the digital divide between older and younger adults can loom large. With this in mind, we will discuss the role technology plays in discrimination.

How a senior interacts with technology has proven to be a complex subject, since that interaction is usually highly personal rather than prescriptive. A senior's relationship with technology—whether it be the internet, email or a smartphone—is interesting from a body-language perspective and depends on their capacity to feel comfortable with it. We will explore the impact of technology on a senior's body language in greater detail in Chapter Nine.

Making decisions about which technology to use is not always easy. You may ask, "What do I buy? A computer or a tablet? Or both?" Society is surrounded by an array of technology, with gadgets powered by AI comprising a big part of this. What is the most suitable gadget for your needs? Will it be easy to use? What is the benefit to you? How will it make your life better?

Arguably, technology almost seems to have become a religion to some people. They remain glued to their smartphones for hours on end, checking emails and social media. It's gotten to the point where society as a whole can't survive without technology, with the constant nagging fear of a cyberattack, whether it be on a stock exchange, government department, company or organization, looming in the background. If seniors are less keen to embrace technology, including AI, than their younger counterparts, even though they may benefit from doing so, this might be due to a lack of trust, leading to concerns regarding security and privacy.

Fear is a big psychological problem to overcome. People may be afraid they will make costly mistakes if they embrace technology. They may have wider concerns too. For example: is adopting a particular technology socially responsible? These are among the myriad reasons why some older people are rejecting digital technologies, so rest assured we will discuss these and other issues at length.

AI has significant implications for a country's national income, either increasing or decreasing it. The way we live and work is becoming more and more flexible and hybrid. For this reason, AI has an impact on the macro-economics of not only a country, but the whole world.

Technology could be good for ensuring democracies either endure or are created. By using technology in the right way, we can level the playing field between rich and poor and between those who have power and those who do not. As United States politician and former chief executive officer (CEO) of Hewlett Packard, Carly Fiorina, says:

> "You know, I believe that technology is the great leveler… it's not only a great tool for democratization, but it's a great tool for eliminating prejudice and advancing meritocracies."[4]

Of course, we cannot be certain of the role technology will have in achieving a level playing field, but there are positive signs. We can only hope. Seniors have an important role to play in making this happen.

Current paradigms must change and this book will play its part in changing them. You will be able to dip in and out of the chapters as you require more information about certain areas. If you embrace technology, you may be able to lead a more independent life, stay in the workforce for longer or be more successful in taking up a new career than those seniors who don't. You may even choose to become an entrepreneur. Overall, technology has the potential to ensure you lead a long, healthy and rewarding life, whatever your age.

PART ONE

COMMON CONCERNS ABOUT TECHNOLOGY

Our world is shaped by many things, from the political to the social and, of course, technology. AI is important in that shaping. When writing this book, we learned that many seniors, unfortunately, are not only shunning information technology (IT) and its benefits, but they don't even know what it is. Without sufficient knowledge and understanding about technology, it is no wonder that seniors may fear it and avoid using it. When you are more knowledgeable, you will feel more comfortable with IT and fear it less.

In Part One, we will look at where we humans are now in our relationship with IT and how things might look in the future. Chapter One will examine technologies that we use every day and the benefits of doing so. Often, these technologies are powered by AI, but most people don't even know that.

Chapter Two will deal with the rights and wrongs of AI. AI-powered gadgets are becoming increasingly important in the take up—or not—of new technology by seniors and the rest of society, which is why the ethical implications of AI matter. This is especially true when it comes to issues like climate change and sustainability, which have huge impacts on societal attitudes.

AI also has implications for factors such as the job market. Will there be more or fewer jobs as a result of AI? Will more people be looking for jobs? How will AI affect younger generations?

One of the things we (the authors) learned while carrying out our research for this book is that if seniors want to feel more comfortable around AI and how it is used, then they need to know more about it. Lack of knowledge often manifests itself in fear of the unknown, which is a powerful emotion. We will focus on how to deal with the fear of technology in the last chapter of Part One, entitled "What If I Get It Wrong?"

1

What Are All These Technologies?

Everyone, not just seniors, is likely to be using AI-driven technology every day. IT, and AI in particular, is around us all the time, whether we live in a retirement village or independently. It pervades nearly everything we do and has a profound effect on our lives, but most of the time, we don't even know it.

There is no need to worry if you are unsure whether your device is powered by AI. Lots of people, even younger ones, don't know this. It seems that some young people aren't as tech-savvy as older people may think. That said, the extent to which someone knows about technology often depends on when they were born. The Millennials tend to pick up technology relatively quickly, while those known as Generation Z are "digital natives." In other words, they not only do everything online, but they expect to do it that way. In extreme cases, some young people don't even interact in person; instead, they prefer to get likes on social media. Whether these people have benefited from technology is debatable, but most of us, including seniors, have definitely benefited from it.

The devices that we use can be anything from a cell phone, voice recognition device or computer to one that operates the lights and heating, refrigerator, oven or television. Today, for example, it is common for refrigerators to alert users when they leave the door open too long. Many refrigerators and ovens are also self-cleaning. In this way, AI is being used to create a smart home for the benefit of everyone.

Technology, and AI in particular, powers everything from personalized websites to chatbots. It makes automated tagging possible to track luggage that goes missing on an airline flight or everyday items that get lost. AI enables people to have illnesses diagnosed more quickly and those who have a disability to lead full and independent lives. People who are visually impaired, for example, can use smartphones that describe their surroundings or have extra big buttons. In the future, smartphones are likely to have long-lasting batteries to reduce their carbon footprint, benefiting the environment as well as humans.

Throughout the Covid-19 pandemic of 2020–2021, video technology like Zoom, Skype or Google Meet enabled people to stay in touch with their families and friends while self-isolating and during the lockdowns. Consequently, many older people became more accustomed to and comfortable with using technology to speak with their children and grandchildren. In this sense, the pandemic was a catalyst for technological adoption and change.

As a consequence of video technology, the way we use our body to communicate with other people has changed. Speaking on screen is very different than face-to-face interaction, and our body language must change and adapt accordingly. All the senses play a part in digital body language and robots programmed by AI can read this language. As a result, our traditional body-language skills must adapt so we can create influence and impact on screen. Modern body-language skills require an approach that includes our screen presence and the need to create an instant rapport with our audience.

Although you may find having to adjust your body language to deal with technological change somewhat confusing, continued interaction with technology will make this easier. You will learn more about how body language is impacted by technology in Chapter Nine. As a starting point and to help to reduce any fear you may have around technology, particularly AI, this chapter aims to give you more information about what AI is and some of the ways in which it is being used to benefit everyone, including seniors.

What is AI?

The simplest definition of AI is "intelligence demonstrated by machines, as opposed to the natural intelligence displayed by humans or animals."[1] The term was coined in 1956[2] and is described by the *Oxford Dictionary of English* as "the theory and development of computer systems able to perform tasks normally requiring human intelligence, such as visual perception, speech recognition, decision-making, and translation between languages."[3]

To be clear, robotics and AI are two different disciplines. Some robots are programmed to perform human functions without AI, but others are programmed with AI. When AI is used, robots can emulate the human mind and follow human actions. An example would be Amazon's Astro "Alexa on Wheels" home robot, which performs household tasks.[4]

AI comprises of several disciplines such as data processing and machine learning. Algorithms are created, classifying, analyzing and drawing predictions from large datasets. With AI, it's usually possible to do more in less time than it would take a human.

AI is expected to become the most transformative technology that humanity has ever seen. For example, it will be important in meeting the requirements of the Fourth Industrial Revolution (4.0) where physical assets and advanced digital technologies, such as the internet of things (IoT), robots, drones, autonomous vehicles, 3D printing, cloud computing and nanotechnology, communicate, analyze and act on the information they gather. This enables organizations, consumers and society to be more flexible and responsive to demands and make intelligent data-driven decisions.[5]

There are different types of AI.[6] The first is reactive AI, which is the oldest and most limited form. Nonetheless, it can still respond to various stimulations in the same way as the human mind does. In 1997, IBM's supercomputer Deep Blue, a reactive AI machine, beat chess grandmaster Garry Kasparov.[7]

The next type is limited memory AI. As well as having the capabilities of purely reactive machines, this type of AI can learn from historical data to make decisions. Nearly all existing applications that we know of, such as chatbots, personal assistants (PAs) and digital fingerprinting, come under this category of AI.

"Theory of mind" and "self-aware" are two types of AI that are at the conceptual or hypothetical stage. The aim is that the machine will possess an adequate amount of self-awareness to emulate the human brain. It is possible for an entity like this to become more powerful than any human being.[8]

Artificial narrow intelligence (ANI) refers to AI systems that can only perform a specific task autonomously using human-like capabilities, but you would still know it is a robot. It uses training data and learning experiences from previous incidents. Most AI currently used fits in this category. An AI agent that uses artificial general intelligence (AGI) is more developed than ANI. This type of agent can learn, perceive, understand and function completely like a human being in a way that is more than "human-like capabilities." It is a human! The most super-intelligent AGI is still evolving.[9]

Finally, artificial superintelligence (ASI) means that AI-powered agents are likely to be more intelligent than the brightest and most gifted human minds. When AI reaches this stage, IT developers and the human species as a whole will certainly need to take ethical concerns into account.[10]

What is the impact of AI?

Here are a few examples of how we are currently using AI:[11]

- Smartphone or PC digital PAs

- Web search

- Machine translations

- Cybersecurity

- Fighting disinformation

- Optimizing products and sales paths

- Smart air conditioning

- IoT, for example smart vacuum cleaners, refrigerators, ovens, televisions or watches

- Autonomous cars

- Online shopping and advertising

- Smart farming

- Robots used in factories

Another use of AI is in video games. For the most part, video games focus on responsive, adaptive and interactive AI-powered experiences that are usually generated via non-player characters. Take the movie *Free Guy*, for example.[12] The main character, Guy, lives in Free City, but he doesn't exist in reality. He only exists in a video game where the same things happen at the same time every day. It can be confusing to watch, but for anyone interested in learning more about AI, it is worth seeing.

The other type of AI in video games is when the main character has some memory of what has happened before and adjusts its thoughts, behaviors and actions accordingly. This is the more popular view of AI in this context.

AI is important in the business world and is predicted to be the biggest commercial growth area in the next few years. If all businesses were to adopt AI, global gross domestic product (GDP) would advance by 14% by 2030—that's about US$15 trillion.[13]

It's no surprise, therefore, that big companies are taking advantage of AI. For example, Amazon, which has its foundations in AI, generates 35% of its revenue from its recommendation engine.[14] Smaller businesses, however, are not taking up AI to the same extent, despite the fact that it is likely to be beneficial.

When it comes to finance, people can track their wealth more easily by using AI for accounting and problem-solving. Accounting software combines AI and cloud computing, which we will discuss in more detail in Chapter Five on wealth.

AI in retail and fashion

With the help of AI, grocery and fashion shopping is being made easier for everyone, especially seniors. You can stay at home if you wish and surf the internet for whatever you want to buy, and items are usually delivered to the door within days by courier. In the future, drones, which use AI technology, are likely to deliver goods instead of human couriers. It will also become possible to consult with robots as well as humans to enhance the shopping experience.

If you're shopping instore, you will have to get used to your eyes being monitored and receiving marketing material based on what you look at. Although retailers have been watching people's eye movements for years—they can tell if you like the product, love it or are indifferent to it from signals in your facial expression and eyes—through facial recognition, retailers can get customers to buy exactly what is on their minds. All recommendations can be more personalized.

Many retail businesses that have embraced AI are growing rapidly as a result. Amazon, for example, has used AI extensively to build its ecommerce business, making recommendations for video and music streaming. It has also deployed AI at Amazon Go cashier-less grocery stores. On September 1, 2021, it opened a contactless grocery store in Dalston, East London, called Amazon Fresh, using "Just Walk Out" technology. It's the retailer's sixth convenience store in London. This automatically detects when products are taken from or returned to the shelves and keeps track of them in a virtual basket, so when customers have finished shopping, they can just leave the store. Their Amazon account is then charged and a receipt is sent by email.[15]

The global lockdowns due to the Covid-19 pandemic meant online shopping really took off, but AI is not just about getting your weekly groceries. It can also help in predicting fashion trends and reducing wastage, enabling a company to be more environmentally friendly. The creation of avatars and the introduction of virtual reality (VR), augmented reality (AR) and the metaverse are making it easy to come to decisions about what to buy to wear.

What is the metaverse? Two words, meta and universe, have been put together to create metaverse, a buzzword for several technologies that facilitate a more interactive 3D experience. AR and VR are often used in the metaverse, making it an immersive visual experience on the internet where you can try on clothes with your own "personal shopper" having your measurements and other shopping data. Since there is virtual sizing, the likelihood of returns is reduced.

Fashion stylists are also entering the metaverse and you could benefit from using them when shopping online. Gemma Sheppard was the first fashion "global director" to use the metaverse, teaming up with UK-based investment firm Metaventures and the gaming platform Roblox, and using virtual models.[16]

The world's first digital supermodel was computer-generated Shudu Gram.[17] She hit Instagram in 2017 and has courted controversy ever since because she is a black woman created by a twenty-eight-year-old-white man. Despite this, she is used by some designers to demonstrate their products, Rihanna's makeup range being one of them. Shudu has generated a following of about 220,000 people on Instagram.

Other computer-generated models are Lil Miquela, who is Spanish, Brazilian and American;[18] Lightning, who is Japanese;[19] and Noonouri, who was created by a German, but lives in Paris.[20] They are virtual influencers and have thousands of followers on social media, where they post images of themselves wearing garments or carrying handbags from their favorite designers.

The introduction of AI into fashion, which has been considered to be one of the world's most polluting industries, has helped it to become more environmentally friendly. At present, the fashion industry is the second-biggest consumer of water and is responsible for 8–10% of global carbon emissions.[21] It is such a big user of water because it needs a lot for crops like cotton, while oil-based pesticides, machinery for harvesting and transport of goods account for the emissions. The United Nations Alliance for Sustainable Fashion, launched in March 2019, is seeking to halt these practices.[22]

By winning the hearts and minds of those who are environmentally concerned, including seniors, AI is likely to be more readily embraced by this group. Many seniors are waste conscious and seek environmentally friendly solutions. Virtual models not only help designers show their latest creations worldwide, they also help to reduce waste by showcasing clothes that haven't actually been manufactured.

Several companies are using technology to make fashion more eco-friendly and sustainable. Heuritech, a market intelligence platform based in Paris, France, is one.[23] It forecasts products and trends, saying that by using AI, it can reduce overall inventory levels by 20% to 50% and improve labor conditions.

AI can help fashion brands predict trends, including colors and fabrics, and design their products accordingly. It can also make forecasting less labor intensive, reducing the need for fashion designers and influencers to spend time in manual or digital observation and data collection. A company that has developed software to aid fashionistas in their forecasting is Stylumia, based in India.[24] It has developed a consumer intelligence tool that analyzes data using AI-powered technology to help fashion and lifestyle brands forecast demand, spot trends, manage inventory and make better business decisions generally. More accurate forecasting will help cut wastage, which grows at over 70 billion garments a year, according to Stylumia's website.[25]

Transportation

Access to transport is a key issue faced by seniors, who may be struggling with declining eyesight, hearing, reflexes and mobility. Many companies have developed or are developing AI solutions for cars—degrees of autonomous vehicle devices (AVDs)—so that seniors have greater independence and more mobility when they're outside their homes. There is more about AVDs and how they can benefit seniors in Chapter Eight.

In 2018, the US-based Consumer Technology Association (CTA) Foundation, Local Motors, a car company in Arizona, USA, and IBM Accessibility Research teamed up to develop autonomous vehicles to help people who are struggling with accessibility.[26] As a result, Olli, a self-driving electric 3D-printed minibus that can carry up to eight people, was launched with the aim of helping seniors stay mobile and independent. Olli is equipped with advanced vehicle technology, including IBM Watson IoT for Automotive so that the vehicle and the passenger can talk with one another. It has begun operating and is being trialed by several cities around the world, including Amsterdam in the Netherlands.[27]

Abu Dhabi's Masdar City has also developed a driverless bus that can transport about twelve people.[28] Masdar City was started in 2006 by Mubadala Investment Company, the country's sovereign wealth fund, and is attracting partners from all over the world to innovate and develop transport solutions. Seniors will, of course, benefit from these solutions. If these vehicles are carbonless, as is the case with Masdar City, then there will be even more benefit.

The future

How will the future of AI look? One of the things that could happen is that digital offspring will interact with human children and it will be nearly impossible to tell the difference between the two.[29] Catriona Campbell, a behavioral psychologist and one of the UK's leading authorities on AI and emerging or disruptive technologies, calls digital offspring the "Tamagotchi generation" after the digital pets popular in Japan.[30]

The day will come when we'll all have the option to have chips in our bodies. In fact, this is happening already in Sweden and Japan. These chips are used for electronic payments and to control smartphones. By the time they become commonplace, humans will be better able to relate to and control robots. The CEO of Nokia, Pekka Lundmark, speaking in Davos, Switzerland, said that by 2030, smartphones would become far less common as technology would be wearable or "built directly" into the physical body.[31]

However, even if AI can deliver the types of relevant customized experiences that seniors demand, many people aren't sold on its benefits or adopting it as quickly as may have been expected. Why is this?

Seniors may have ethical concerns about AI. One of those is that AI is inherently biased. Another is that an AI-powered robot doesn't "feel" enough. The ethics of AI is too big a subject to gloss over, so we will discuss it in more depth in the next chapter.

Case study: How technology has changed

Technology has changed a great deal in just a few decades and will keep on changing. I (Lucia Dore) moved from Invercargill (at the bottom of the South Island in New Zealand (NZ)) to London at the beginning of 1989 (January 1, to be exact). I had been an economist at the NZ Treasury and had left to do a post-graduate diploma in journalism at the University of Canterbury. Then I was to head to London and wanted to write to newspapers before I arrived there to secure appointments for my project. At that time, I had to find an office in Invercargill with a computer that would allow me to make multiple copies of the same document. We had no household computer at home; many businesses, including my parents' motel, didn't have a computer, either.

Finally, I found what I needed and mailed the letters to London. There was no such thing as email back then.

When I arrived in London, I purchased a state-of-the-art electronic typewriter. That was in the mid-80s. Using that, I was able to complete my research while working. I had an office administration job on a temporary basis initially and then I worked for a new-launch weekly magazine.

There, we used Amstrad computers, which were pretty rudimentary compared to the tasks the computers can do now. They didn't even have a word count facility, which was tricky when it came to writing articles. Copy was saved on clunky floppy disks. Faxes were used, all the time, and seemed very high tech. I sent letters via fax from London to Invercargill.

Technology has certainly moved on since the mid-1980s. People are now reliant on email, and faxes have been phased out. Computers are also much more sophisticated now. Emails are not only used all the time, they are relied on.

Now too, nearly everyone owns a smartphone which has more memory than the old Amstrad computers ever did. When it comes to saving a document, instead of using a clunky floppy disk, everything is either saved to the cloud or to a USB stick.

Summary

In this chapter, we have looked at the technology that is around us right now and how things are likely to progress. We have covered:

- What AI is

- The development of IT and AI

- Ways in which we use technology every day

- How technology can enhance the life of seniors

- What the future holds for AI

AI and IT are so integral to our lives now that it's unlikely anyone can imagine a world without them. Even those of us who can remember an era without technology tend to struggle to understand how we coped without our smartphone and the internet, but technology is developing at such a pace that these things one day will become obsolete as new solutions take over.

However, taking over is one thing we as human beings ultimately do not want technology to do. We don't want to be the solution that ends up being obsolete, so there are ethical questions that we all need to ask concerning where AI will take us in the future. That is what we will cover in the next chapter.

2

Is Technology Desirable?

As more governments, companies and organizations are using AI technologies than ever before, ethical issues are arising, all of which need to be considered closely and carefully. It's not only scholars and academics undertaking this scrutiny, but government advisers and politicians, too.

Is AI being deployed in the best interests of society and the individual—seniors in particular? This is just one of the many ethical questions that arise as technology advances in leaps and bounds. This chapter looks at some of these ethical issues in relation to seniors, including whether their independence and privacy will be preserved.

What are AI ethics?

According to the Alan Turing Institute based in the UK, AI ethics are "a set of values, principles, and techniques that employ widely accepted standards of right and wrong to guide moral conduct in the development and use of AI technologies."[1] Since AI is a relatively new area, it is developing all the time, so what is and is not ethical with regards to AI still needs to be figured out.

Some organizations, such as the Arthur W. Page Center at Penn State University,[2] focus on "digital ethics," but there is some debate over its scope. Should digital ethics be determined by a platform such as Google or Amazon, or by the technology that supports it, such as digital video, imagery, games, Word Press, social media, databases or audio?

The use of tracking software raises many concerns, including privacy, data collection and protection, governance, accountability and cybersecurity. Some seniors already fear using technology and this fear is exacerbated by the use of tracking software. Such software is everywhere. Smartphones are tracked, looking at such issues as how long you spend using the device and at what times. To put your mind at rest somewhat, several commentators have documented how to find out if you are being tracked.[3]

Tracking software has its benefits. It makes sure advertisements are personalized to the device user, but the flip side of this is that advertisers can collect more data about customers. The latest iPhone has more security, according to a cyber report on CNBC.[4] It's possible to put your phone in lockdown mode but still receive messages for example. This will give increased comfort to seniors.

The latest smartphones permit people to track their loved ones so they know their whereabouts at all times. This is particularly useful for parents of young children, but this can also be a comfort to seniors who may feel vulnerable going out alone, particularly after dark. Tracking can be done either through sharing a location or on the My Friends app. Ethically, however, this raises issues of dependency and privacy.

You can track your property, whether it is a set of car keys, a wallet or an item of jewelry. If you use an Apple iPhone, you can also track your luggage on an airline. To track your luggage, you must first purchase an AirTag for about US$29. Using Bluetooth technology, the iPhone will then play a sound if your lost luggage is nearby.[5]

What is the ethical question here? There were initially complaints about AirTag being used by stalkers, but in February 2022, Apple issued a statement that it would make changes to AirTag so that it couldn't be used for malicious or criminal purposes.[6]

In the health sector, one ethical issue that could arise regarding tracking is a clash between the needs and wants of a caregiver and an older person. Caregivers may prefer to track older people so that they are aware when they do something unusual, but seniors may not want to be tracked, saying this is an invasion of privacy. Is it really, though, if it is in the best interest of seniors to be tracked so that they can live independent lives, safe in the knowledge that if something goes wrong—they fall, for example—then help will be on its way? Do privacy concerns outweigh a person's health and safety?

Many seniors are concerned about the world economy and AI's impact on the labor market. Do seniors have to leave the workforce or will they be encouraged to stay in it? What do current trends mean for the younger generation? Will the use of AI and robots create more jobs or lead to a reduction?

Designing digital devices for seniors is increasingly regarded as the right thing to do, as we'll see throughout this book (Chapters Four, Five and Seven), but what are the ethical issues around this? Do manufacturers have a bias toward the younger generation when designing devices such as smartphones? Are there particular concerns that seniors have that manufacturers need to take into account when they're designing devices? Can the numbers on smartphones be read easily by older eyes, for example? Do seniors require a technology that is "ethically sound"—ie morally acceptable—more than other age groups? Since many seniors don't like using any kind of technology, how important is this for manufacturers to consider? We will discuss this point in more depth in Chapter Seven.

Is technology always ethical?

Many gadgets that seniors work with daily are powered by AI or machine learning (ML), which are interconnected and have become part of everyday life. Smartphones, which most people have, can be used for timekeeping, improving security or taking photos. They often use facial recognition and global positioning systems (GPS) for navigation.

Targeted AI processors (often called neural processing engines or something similar) are instrumental in enabling AR. Siri (the PA embedded in Apple phones) and Alexa (developed by Amazon) can act as virtual assistants (VAs). The cameras on smartphones are improving all the time, many automatically removing red eye and sorting the photos in different ways, such as by type of place or into albums, rather than only by date. It is also easy to add images, music or emojis to any message sent online, whether it is via social media, messenger or email.

How far should AI go, though? When will it have it gone too far from an ethical perspective? Is the removal of red eye acceptable? Is photoshopping pictures on a computer before they are published ethical?

Other AI-powered gadgets have benefited seniors, such as semi-autonomous vehicles (the precursor to driverless cars), devices to turn the television on and off and channel surf from the armchair, refrigerators that makes a noise when left open or stoves and ovens that alerts the user if they are left on. Retailers, investment companies and healthcare organizations use AI, and nearly all developments have been good for seniors. In 2019, Google introduced a Pixel telephone that could transcribe speech to text and perform other tasks without any connection to the cloud.[7] This will make it easier for some seniors to send text messages, even if they feel their fingers are too big or no longer nimble enough for the keypad.

AI has helped decision makers in areas such as marketing, but is the capturing of data by marketers ethical? What data are they collecting and for what purpose? Do they meet the governance requirements of a particular jurisdiction, primarily in terms of values, principles and protocols? What are the ethical implications for stakeholders and communities? To whom are organizations accountable? Are they even regulated? Seniors need to know the answers to these and many more questions if they are to overcome their fear of using technology, but the failure of companies, organizations, websites and/or governments to be transparent on this matter plays in this fear.

There is also concern about the way AI-powered technology is designed and used, which could have negative consequences on society, particularly since AI is an emerging technology. The Alan Turing Institute points out that it is essential to ensure the design and use of AI protects fundamental human rights.[8] Humans must always have oversight of an AI-powered gadget. They need to be able to step in to control or switch off that gadget if required.

Delivering AI

How AI is delivered matters to society as a whole and to individuals, including seniors, so it's important that the delivery platform is ethically sound. Seniors, among others, need to trust it, but what constitutes an ethical delivery platform?

One framework that can be used is support, underwrite and motivate (SUM), according to the Alan Turing Institute.[9] SUM values comprise of four key concepts: respect, connect, care and protect. The objectives of these values are to provide people with an accessible framework to start thinking about the moral scope of the societal and ethical impacts of a project, and evaluate how a project meets ethical criteria. SUM values ensure a project is ethical by providing an actionable set of principles.

The institute also sets out other principles by which organizations and companies should abide. These are called Fairness, Accountability, Sustainability and Transparency (FAST) Track Principles and aim to provide the practitioner with the tools to make sure that a project is without bias, non-discriminatory and fair. Public trust in a project "to deliver safe and reliable AI innovation" must be certain, the report states, so the Alan Turing Institute sets out a third option, combining both the SUM and FAST principles.

A study in July 2019 by Capgemini Research Institute emphasizes the importance of ensuring public trust when designing and delivering an AI project.[10] It found that "62% [of consumers] said they would place higher trust in a company whose AI interactions they perceived as ethical, 61% said they would share positive experiences with friends and family, 59% said that they would have higher loyalty to the company [that followed ethical practices], and 55% said that they would purchase more products and provide high ratings and positive feedback on social media."

Developers are also looking at the ethical issues that can arise with AI-powered technology. The SAS Institute, a US-based software company, has outlined the key ethical considerations when evaluating an AI solution in a paper.[11] The considerations it highlights are:

- Does the solution deliver fair and equitable outcomes?

- Is the solution in any way either introducing or exacerbating a bias?

- Will the solution being proffered result in humans feeling or experiencing loss of control or agency?

- How will employees be impacted?

Empathy

To understand more about empathy in relation to AI, Pega Systems—a US-based company founded in 1983 that develops software for customer relationship management (CRM), robotic process automation and business process management (BPM)—conducted a survey of 6,000 consumers from North America, the UK, Australia, Japan, Germany and France.[12] It looked specifically at empathy and AI. In this context, empathy was defined as the ability to understand and share the feelings of another, or simply "putting yourself in someone else's shoes." This raises the question as to whether humans are born with empathy or whether it is learned.

Half of the participants believed human beings are born with the capacity for empathy, half that humans must learn or be taught it. That said, of the respondents believing in humans' capacity for empathy, 38% didn't think humans were the best example. In other words, they didn't think CRM personnel, for example, would always act in the best interests of the customer.

The survey looked at the way AI is being used in a number of human interactions, such as with bank managers or customer service operators. According to Pega Systems, 68% of participants would trust a human more than AI to decide on bank loan approvals, while 69% said they would be more inclined to tell the truth to a person than a chatbot powered by AI. From the people we have spoken to while writing this book and the surveys we have undertaken among seniors, we have found that in general, people prefer to deal with a "real person." Since many seniors have more disposal income than younger people, it would behoove banks and other customer service operators to take this into account.

About 40% of respondents in the Pega survey agreed that AI has the potential to improve customer service and customer interaction, but there was considerable concern that AI will take over human jobs and make life more difficult for society. About 35% of respondents said they were concerned about this.

An ethical question surrounding empathy, or lack thereof, concerns spam emails. Based on empirical evidence, we have concluded that such emails show a lack of ethical values. For the most part, they show no empathy with the recipient, no understanding of what the recipient does, what country they live in or the fact that they may not be interested in the product that the sender is trying to sell.

Bias

Bias is another concern with AI, with 54% of respondents in the Pega survey saying that they would expect some bias.[13] The same percentage felt that AI will always make decisions based on the biases of the person who created it and were skeptical about a machine's ability to learn and adapt. Researchers have pointed out that AI can perpetuate biases, such as age-related or gender-related biases.[14] These biases, especially gender-related ones, can be a result of the views of the developer or programmer, who is usually male. For this reason, most of the programming for AI is from a male perspective.

Bias in AI comes into play because AI gathers data and picks up patterns from everyday activities—usually from the male developer perspective. It then correlates the cause and effect based on existing knowledge. But AI has its limits. As management consultant Marc Botha says in his article "The limits of artificial intelligence":

> "When large amounts of data and many factors come together, artificial intelligence is superior to human intelligence. However, only humans can think logically and distinguish between useful and worthless AI advice."[15]

Environmental concerns

Increasingly, people, including seniors, are concerned about climate change and the environmental impact of their activities. What role can AI play in protecting the environment? What role might it play in threatening the planet?

There are two aspects to AI's involvement in the environment. Some AI-powered gadgets, such as driverless cars, are responsible for pollution. AI may mean that people drive more, making the roads more congested and using more energy to charge cars, for example.[16] AI-powered gadgets could help reduce emissions, however, winning the hearts and minds of a huge proportion of the population. Equally, governments might be able to use AI-powered gadgets to help clean up the environment.

Kate Crawford, co-founder of research at the AI Now Institute at New York University, a principal researcher at Microsoft Research, visiting chair for AI and social justice at the École Normale Supérieure in Paris, and an honorary professor at the University of Sydney, looks at some of these issues in her book *Atlas of AI: Power, politics, and the planetary costs of artificial intelligence.*[17] This book shows how "the global networks underpinning AI technology are damaging the environment, entrenching inequality, and fueling a shift toward undemocratic governance." Kate argues that resources must be extracted from people rather the planet and the way AI products are designed and used is biased. Technological systems are designed to give an impression of neutrality, when in fact they serve "existing systems of power."[18]

Deception in AI

The use of AI-powered technology raises important questions about deception. To what extent are AI-powered gadgets and robots deceiving humans? Are we more likely to be deceived if we are older? Are AI gadgets better at detecting deception than humans are?

Case study: Deception is part of everyday life

In my work and research as a global body-language guru and co-founder of Senior Behavioural Shift, I (Carole Railton) have found that in daily interactions, 57% of lies are never detected. Yet humans spend time looking at and understanding how someone lies.

Bots are programmed with all the information I have as a body-language expert, and more, which means they are capable of understanding humans. They already know how we feel, if we are stressed, how to treat us and when we are lying. They could choose either to help us or to put us under more stress.

Just as humans sometimes withhold information to influence an outcome, a robot can do the same to get what it wants. For example, a robot can send incorrect information to deceive a human. While these behaviors can be useful in wartime when the bot is dealing with an enemy, they can be less than helpful in everyday life.

People tend to believe most of what they read, and how they work with systems means their ulterior motive is not questioned. The most common AI control is voice activation, but how do we let it know what to do when something different turns up? What if our voice is muffled and the systems get a different message to the one we are relaying? Although what is happening is not deception per se, the bot is confused (deceived). It has misunderstood the information.

I have found that 93% of people lie; it's part of survival. Even a soldier's camouflage is a form of deceptive behavior, but deception is usually used for altruistic reasons. For example, when you ask a robot: "How do I look in my new coat?" and it answers "Lovely," it is likely that the bot has been programmed to deceive. But not all opinions are deceptive. It is important to assume that bots answer most questions—they are designed to do this. Only when a bot does not recognize a question will it get passed to a human or it will ask for the question to be rephrased.

Given how much information and power robots will have in our lives in the future, it makes sense to look at ways of understanding how we can tell what is going on with them. We need to make sure that they put us under the least amount of risk and deception. AI is already attempting to deceive us.

Some AI is manipulated to deceive on purpose, which can be serious. Deception in this instance can mean the manipulation of audio, video or imagery. As much of AI is pre-programmed, it is important to understand how much before we can propose defenses.

Emmanuel Goffi interview with Lucia Dore, March 30 2022

In my interview with Emmanuel Goffi, philosopher of AI and co-director and co-founder of the Global AI Ethics Institute in Paris, we discussed, among other things, some of the cultural differences around AI. Here, he talks about this issue and what seniors should consider regarding ethics and AI.

Lucia: "How does the Global AI Ethics Institute differ from other institutes around the world?"

Emmanuel: "The institute aims to bring back philosophy when considering AI technologies and take into account the philosophy of all cultures. For example, ethics tends to be a Western construct, but different cultures consider ethics, whether around AI or other issues, differently. This is known as 'contextual ethics.'

"Between about 60% and 70% of the codes of ethics around AI come from the West. Is this right? This affects programming. In the future, China will be a leader in AI. There is also a big dynamic in AI in India. Consequently, the institute wants to ensure a more open philosophical debate about the introduction of AI technologies and products, whether it is within the European Union or other cultures."

Lucia: "What are some of the issues that older people have to deal with when it comes to ethics and AI?"

Emmanuel: "Older people often do not have as much technological knowledge as younger ones, making them more vulnerable to scammers. On top of the information about AI, there is a lack of critical thinking, which is often not taught in schools or universities. The institute is all about critical thinking and understanding what can be done.

"When it comes to training, we need more emphasis on those who don't have much knowledge about AI. Lack of training is currently causing a problem for seniors."

This meant that seniors do not embrace technology to the extent that they should, he said, and often fall prey to scammers.

Summary

In this chapter, we have looked at a number of concerns surrounding whether we should be using AI at all, including:

- How ethical is AI?

- What are the biases that AI could perpetuate?

- Can AI be used to enhance the environment, or does it do more harm than good?

- Are AI ethics global?

It is critical that governments and organizations are transparent when it comes to their use of AI. Many people, and particularly seniors who may not have as much technological knowledge as their younger counterparts, mistrust what they don't understand, and a lack of transparency will only perpetuate the fear of the unknown. Entities such as the Global AI Ethics Institute aim to address the concerns we have covered in this chapter, which is certainly a step in the right direction.

In the last chapter of Part One, we will take a closer look at the fear that many seniors feel when confronted by a whole new digital world.

3

What If I Get
It Wrong?

Given the fact that everyone reacts differently to technology, it is not surprising that discussions about how older people will interact with IT are many and varied. Often, though, problems that seniors encounter with technology are a result of a lack of confidence born from a fear of using the latest gadget.

This chapter will look at that fear and lack of confidence that often surrounds seniors using technology. We will discuss how this fear might manifest itself and how to overcome it, because enjoying technology matters.

Reactions to using technology

Mike Collins, CEO of Business South in New Zealand and former Director of Learning Environment (Technology & Facilities) and Director Service Excellence at Otago Polytechnic, outlined the reactions of seniors to technology in a recent exclusive interview. In it, he talked about a survey that was undertaken by Otago Polytechnic that touched upon how seniors use technology.[1]

Mike Collins Interview with Lucia Dore, April 12 2022

"We found that in the fifty to sixty age group, some embraced technology. About 10% were first followers; the rest needed a lot of mentoring and support. AI was a mystery for many people, and many more were struggling with social media."

Fifteen years ago, Mike told me, older people tended to have a lot of fear around AI and robotics, particularly whether they would benefit and make a positive difference to their lives. Now there is less fear, especially since AI is being used for social causes such as preventing climate change.

"This wins the hearts and minds of people," he noted. "Big organizations around the world are using smart technologies and innovating to make a difference to the world.

"The speed of change has picked up. Some older people—such as those in their mid-seventies—are often surprised at the benefits they can get from technology. Rather than fear, there is more curiosity about new technologies. There is a question of 'What's next?'

"Seniors are realizing that AI and robotics can benefit them. For example, self-driving cars and lawnmowers using AI not only make life easier for seniors, they can also save time. Increasingly, machines are being used in the market and people are beginning to build up trust that these machines can make a difference to their lifestyle."

Some seniors, Mike said, are happy to learn how to use new technology. They argue that they were at the forefront of technology from the outset—they built it and made it work for the generations to come, so they are willing to embrace new technology, learn how to handle its myriad changes and enjoy the benefits it can bring.

In contrast, some older people reject technology altogether. There are numerous reasons for this, but it may be that they do not feel the need to use technology because they have always managed without it. "Why change old ways?" they ask.

He believed that more seniors were starting to embrace technology and wanted to do so more but this was difficult since many felt there was a lack of training available. He believed all training institutes have a role to play in this regard.

Frustration

Seniors may feel frustrated if they do not get a response from a link, whether on a cell phone, a desktop or a tablet, thinking that this proves the technology is useless. They seldom consider it may be human error.

Seniors often become frustrated too when they have to learn to use Apple's Siri and Amazon's Alexa, which utilize voice technology. Both have become ubiquitous VAs. Speaking to a gadget often seems uncomfortable especially when that was never the case until relatively recently. These devices use AI, but each is not AI in itself. If you need to know something—for example, if you are traveling somewhere and get lost—you can ask Alexa or Siri. They will send a relevant response back to the device, but they won't be able to work if there is no internet. A more reliable solution in the asking for directions example would be to have GPS fitted in your car. This works alongside AI to give you a better navigational experience.

Both Siri and Alexa have their quirks, which can cause frustration for people of any age. Siri often interrupts when you are having a conversation with someone else on your digital device, whether via telephone, FaceTime or a Zoom call.

"How can I help?" she says when you aren't even talking to her directly. Some elderly users have told Lucia that they have stopped using Alexa because they fear she is recording all their conversations.

A huge source of frustration is the plethora of passwords we need to use with technology. Much of the security for different websites, including online banking, uses complicated passwords that are difficult for a hacker to guess, but easy for the user to forget. Although best practice is to use a different password for every site we visit, most people don't because remembering them all, and which one works which site, is impossible.

A survey conducted in 2019 by HYPR in the US and Canada showed that 78% of respondents forgot their passwords for a personal account and had to reset them within 90 days. For a business account, about 57% of personnel reset their passwords.[2]

Passwords are too easy to forget or lose, and the problem is compounded when a parent dies, leaving their surviving spouse or relatives with no access to their accounts, as Lucia discovered when her father died. Getting into accounts—banks or investments, for example—proved to be very difficult. However, AI can help to recover passwords. Some techniques entail randomly trying out lots of different combinations; another approach is by extrapolating new passwords from previous leaked passwords.[3]

Control

Seniors may be unwilling to embrace technology because they believe that people do not always control it. This is particularly the case with AI. The truth is, any failure to control technology is down to a lack of information on the part of the user.

Take online learning, for example, which is now commonplace. Although users have to be more disciplined with their time to reap the benefits of online learning, ultimately, they can determine when and what to learn. In other words, thanks to AI and IT, they have *more* control over when and where they learn, not less.

Another example is the health sector. There are many IT gadgets to help us look after our health, which gives us more control than ever before. All we need to do is accept a paradigm shift from leaving everything to do with our health in the hands of the medical profession.

Social responsibility

Many seniors reject digital technology because they believe this to be the socially responsible thing to do. They think that if they shop locally—socializing with friends at the coffee shop, for example— their town center remains quirky and interesting and, more importantly, stays afloat.

Rejecting technology completely can lead to problems. One example of a difficulty that is likely to arise for seniors who are not technologically savvy is that there are plans for all rail ticket offices in the UK, which currently issue paper tickets, to be closed.[4] It was announced in June 2022 that all paper tickets would be phased out in a move expected to save the rail companies £500 million annually.

This decision will be fine for those who are accustomed to using the internet, but for those who are not—an estimated 3 million people in the UK, according to Age UK—life will be more difficult.[5] Many more don't have access to a mobile device, Age UK estimates. This is just one of the many reasons why familiarizing yourself with technology and overcoming any fear you may have of using it is essential if you're to enjoy your future.

What is fear?

Research shows that fear triggers both emotional and biochemical responses.[6] There are also good times and bad times to trigger fear. It may be good to experience a rush of fear hormones when you're watching a horror movie, but it's less good when you're dealing with technology. Biochemically, if you're afraid, the same chemicals go to your brain as if you were participating in an extreme activity—bungee jumping or skydiving, for example.

Fear may manifest through an increased heartbeat, shortness of breath and/or a rise in blood pressure. It can even lead to brain fog. However, fear only becomes a phobia if it interferes with our everyday lives. Technophobia—an extreme fear of technology[7]—will increasingly interfere with our ability to do anything as the world gets more and more digital.

Whether you display physical signs or not, it is likely that you will feel apprehensive dealing with technology, new or otherwise, if you haven't encountered it before. Not dealing with technology, though, will make your life difficult. This is especially true of everyday things, such as using a laptop computer or a smartphone, but as we have seen, it is also true in areas such as buying train tickets.

If you don't currently use technology, it does not mean that you are incompetent or stupid. It is important to remember that.

Everyone can find technology complicated and scary, sometimes even younger people. It is normal, but fear—or the symptoms of fear—can be overcome or dealt with. This naturally goes a long way toward helping you cope with it.

Everyone experiences fear at one time or another, but usually for different reasons. It is a natural reaction to different types of stimuli and is our way to protect ourselves. It is normal to feel fear sometimes, but many people *expect* to feel fear.

Older people have grown up in a different era. We've lived through a time when society was less dependent on technology, but the reasons why we may fear it can be complex.

Some seniors are not used to working with a particular type of technology. They may feel traumatized by the difficulties they have had with technology in the past or have "fear memories" of huge and complicated primitive computers.[8] Technology has moved on from that. It is much simpler than it used to be. "Plug and play" means exactly what it says: a gadget is simply plugged in and played.

Not all fear is real. False or viprit fear is when you fear something bad will happen when in actual fact, nothing will happen.[9] That's what often occurs with technology.

As we know, fear can turn into a phobia when it happens all the time. Research shows there are three reactions when a person is confronted by their phobia: flight, fight or freeze.[10] To counter these anxiety-related reactions, particularly the freezing, people often take medication, but the University of Bristol has found that medication may not be beneficial.[11] In fact, it may be the opposite: the study shows that medication can cause harmful side effects. A better understanding of how the brain works and how fear works within the brain is crucial for overcoming anxiety and phobias.

Fear, particularly that which leads to an unwillingness to embrace technology, often manifests itself in a lack of confidence. The fear of the unknown—uncertainty about the future—is powerful. It comes about when we believe we have a lack of power or control. We can only benefit from dealing with our fears, whether they are rational or not.

Research into overcoming fear, particular when it comes to technology, reveals several things that seniors need to do.[12] We need to take our time; we should not feel compelled to rush to keep up with other people. We need to be cognizant of the fact that trying out a technology more than once before we get the hang of it is fine; in fact, it is probably more normal than many of us may think.[13] It's also fine if we have to call an expert in to help us, an "expert" in this context being anyone who knows more about what to do with technology than we do.

Another way to overcome fear is visualization. Anyone who is a technophobe can visualize themselves working with a digital device and being fine doing so. Although fear can make our brain foggy— in other words, we can't think straight and tend to forget things— visualization techniques can overcome this.

Seniors may take a course to learn about the latest technology, whether online, in a learning center or a mixture of both. You can find a summary of some of the courses available in the "Help and support" page. Younger relatives may also be involved in teaching seniors about technology. Seniors tend to respond better to adopting new technology if they are taught by relatives rather than by strangers.

Not learning about and embracing new technology can make it much harder for you to re-enter the workforce, if this is what you plan for later life. It also makes it harder to stay in the job market or change jobs. We will discuss this and the problem of discrimination in more depth in a later chapter.

Although there is little research on the impact of technology and AI on older workers, one paper published in early 2021 in *Organizational Psychology Review* explores this.[14] The paper looks at the intersection of aging and technology, analyzing AI, robotics and automation in work settings and the expected impact of these technologies on older workers.

The paper found what empirical evidence suggests: that the risk of job loss or being pushed into early retirement is higher for low-skilled older workers than it is for those who are highly skilled. Even highly skilled workers are vulnerable, though. According to the authors' data, about 55% of adults aged fifty-five to sixty-five do not have knowledge of basic information and communications technology (ICT), such as the ability to use, solve problems with and collaborate via a computer or tablet or new software.[15] Only 10% of adults aged fifty-five to sixty-five can complete new multiple-step ICT tasks, compared with 42% of adults aged twenty-five to fifty-four.

Some of the concerns that seniors have about using technology are highlighted in this case study from eighty-nine-year-old Anne Mayer Bird.[16]

Case study: Fear and seniors

I worked successfully as an arts and theatre publicist for many years. I got my first job in 1967 when I arrived in the United Kingdom from the United States, weathering many changes in the industry over the years, including the major switch from typewriters to computers. These changes may have affected my working life, but not my daily life, over which I kept a good and firm control.

Almost simultaneously, I lost my husband of many years and endured the shutdown caused by Covid-19. I was trapped in my home by a world I could not manage, where familiar and trustworthy people disappeared. My daughters insisted I should have a sophisticated Apple cell phone, but I still do not know how to use it. Apple does run courses, but they were discontinued during the pandemic.

My GP surgery also closed down and I was expected only to contact my doctor online or via NHS online services. I am pretty fit for my age, but have suffered a failed hip replacement and experience severe vertigo without any medical assistance from my GP. I had already had my jabs, thank goodness.

I do have a landline, but it leaves me very open to fraud and I am reliably told it will soon be phased out. Bank branches are also to be phased out, so I will only be able to bank online via an app. It feels like *everything* will soon be done via my phone.

I live in Hackney where services are all online, even though they're totally unreliable. Silly things like new parking permits or green garbage bags are almost impossible to obtain. I pay, and then wait for weeks while nothing is delivered or dealt with.

I woke up suddenly one night during the summer and realized how frightened I am. I'm alone in the house and vulnerable in so many ways. Even the ways I can help myself, like installing a new and more efficient burglar alarm, involve no other human. I long for the human voice in my life and it isn't there. This progress in the name of technology is all so inexorable, it's like being strapped to a vehicle speeding into a dark tunnel in which there is no end in sight, nor ever will be. Thank goodness I have given up driving before driverless cars become commonplace.

I am elderly, but I am bright, university educated and with full mental powers. Physically, I'm able to manage my steep stairs and do much of my housework, and I'm totally organized in terms of diary, friends, money management and so forth. When I complain to my grown-up daughters about my fear of the modern high-tech world, they all count off the attributes and say, "Everyone knows how to use phones and apps and all the rest of it. What is wrong with you?"

It's a hard question to answer, but I know that *fear* plays a huge role. Probate that followed my husband's death was an extended and complex process during the lockdown, even though I hired an adviser to guide me through a lot of financial complexities I did not understand. I wonder if a new profession might now emerge where people are paid to help those like me, who see the range of online services as lethal rather than helpful. I heard a radio presenter joke the other day about babies being born with cell phones already in their hands, which adds to the attitude often expressed to me that the world is as it is, so I should stop moaning and just get on with it. In other words, the world is not going to turn back, ever, to the comfortable and personal one I remember.

After both my youngest daughter and I lost our husbands almost at the same time, we wrote two books together about grief. The latter was an update on *Good Grief: Embracing life at the time of death*, published by HarperCollins.[17] We received calls and emails and, in her case, dozens of Facebook messages. Most of these messages were from older women and what came through forcefully was not grief, but fear. The person with whom they'd shared their worries was no longer there and no one else seemed to be, either. I am good at advising on grief, but what can I tell a frightened widow about fear when I am also afraid?

Anne Mayer Bird is a publicist and writer. During her career in the UK, she worked for leading arts flagships including Opera North, the National Theatre, the Royal Court Theatre, the Young Vic, the Philharmonia Orchestra and London Contemporary Dance Theatre at The Place. She also had a twenty-year freelance career working for smaller companies. She has written two books since her husband died in 2019.

Summary

In this, the final chapter of Part One, we have looked at the fear so many seniors hold around technology and AI. We have discussed:

- What fear is

- Why we feel fear

- Why we may fear technology

- How we can deal with fear

Even false fear can feel all too real, especially when it is preventing us from moving forward with our lives. It's essential that we arm ourselves with the knowledge to take control of any fear we may feel toward technology so that as the world moves into the future, we move with it.

Taking control is the theme of the next part of the book, in which we will learn how to do so with technology.

PART TWO

TAKING CONTROL OF TECHNOLOGY

The second part of this book looks at how we as seniors interact with and control technology, and how it can benefit us. It focuses on three areas: health, wealth and day-to-day living. We will learn not only how technological developments have created new products that have made it easier for seniors to live more independently, but also the benefits of embracing this technology.

Technology can enhance the lives of seniors in so many ways, especially in relation to home help, healthcare and banking. Issues with mobility, dementia and memory loss, failing sight and hearing, and loneliness are all areas where people may need support as they get older. AI helps in this respect with telemedicine becoming ever more common.

Over the last 100 years, life expectancy has grown. It now ranges from fifty-three years in the Central African Republic to nearly eighty-five years in Japan. In Spain, Switzerland, Italy and Australia, the average life expectancy is eighty-three years.[1]

Many people are dependent on digital services and devices, such as smartphones, social media, email and computers. This gives rise to the question: are humans controlling technology or is technology controlling humans? Philosopher Martin Heidegger argues that it is the latter. In his book, *The Question Concerning Technology And Other Essays*, he states that it is not humans who shape technology, but technology that shapes humans.[2] We (the authors) would respond by saying that knowledge is power. If seniors arm themselves with knowledge on how to use and understand new technology, realize the many benefits it can bring them and keep up to date with developments, there is no doubt that they will be the ones in control. The benefits, among other things, are what Part Two is all about.

According to the UN, one in six (16%) of people in the world will be over sixty-five by 2050.[3] That will be up from one in eleven (9%) in 2019. The UN report says that in 2019, there were 703 million persons aged sixty-five years or over. This is projected to double to 1.5 billion by 2050.

The growing number of older people in all societies has huge implications for private and public spending. This includes the amount of money needed by the government to cover pensions, healthcare and education. In the longer term, economic growth will be impacted. Are more or fewer older people needed in the workforce?

We will discuss these issues in greater depth in Part Two.

4

Technology, Health And Safety

A s a result of technology—AI-powered gadgets in particular—seniors are in a better place than ever before to maintain their health and safety. Technology—from tracking devices to smart refrigerators and convection cookers—is increasingly enabling seniors to look after themselves and caregivers to look after seniors, whether it is used in retirement villages, care homes or traditional homes across the world.

Healthcare incorporates telemedicine: smart platforms that integrate electronic medical records (EMRs) and health records, as well as everything else that makes it easy to monitor health, with AI and analytics. We will discuss how AI is being used in healthcare extensively in this chapter, including a case study that describes some of the benefits of technology and telemedicine.

Empowering seniors to stay healthy

AI is developing quickly. It will become ever smarter and be able to analyze an increasingly large amount of data, but most advancements will happen in developed or rich societies. In these societies, AI will be used more and more in healthcare for seniors, especially in the residential care sector. This could be driven by several factors such as a shortage of caregivers, an aging population and families wanting their senior members to stay in their own homes for as long as possible. Eldercare bots, mental-health bots and companion bots are all already in use and are developing all the time.

Since the turn of the century, the enhancement of medical care has come on in leaps and bounds. Even the sickest of people can live longer than they once did. AI and robotics are transforming healthcare, ensuring that people stay healthy into their senior years, reducing the need for hospitalization and care homes.

Hospitals have ever more sophisticated equipment for monitoring the heart, the chest, blood pressure and many other things. Robots can support seniors in managing illness and injuries via sensors on the body. For example, AI devices are evolving that can predict and prevent falls. If seniors feel secure in the knowledge that help will arrive whenever they need it, they can be confident about living alone.

At the simplest level, AI chatbots at home can help patients keep on top of care plans. These AI applications remind seniors when to take medication, keep doctors' appointments, even when to eat, which helps in removing the anxiety and confusion that many older people face. AI-powered social robots provide a level of companionship for lonely seniors, who may form a relationship with chatbots.

The use of AI applications in communities such as retirement villages is having a profound impact on many lives, with equipment to monitor everyday activities. For example, in a retirement village in Queenstown, New Zealand (where Lucia lived for a time), a dependent senior can wear an AI-powered monitor chain that assures their carer and family members that they are where they're meant to be and that all is well. If a senior behaves unusually or something untoward happens, the AI monitor calls an ambulance. If the monitor is unplugged, a person in another part of the country promptly tells you to plug it back in. The assumption is that people in the villas (as they are called) can do this themselves and do not have a carer.

Seniors are making use of everyday technology to feel safe in an ever-connected world. Recently, a friend told us how her mother had alerted another family member of her fall in the car park of a hospital (coincidence) using an Apple Watch, which is advertised as the "ultimate device for a healthy life."[1] Wearing the watch allowed her to contact her sister immediately. Wearable devices such as the Apple Watch and Fitbit also make it possible to keep track of heartrate, the number of steps taken each day, stress levels and sleep patterns.

Telemedicine will likely become part of all medical treatments. It has not only made it easier than ever before to get medical prescriptions (see the case study later in the chapter), but it can deliver different types of teachings for a healthy life. For example, it can recommend exercises to improve posture. Our posture is changing with technology.[2]

Increasing lifespan and detecting disease

All these developments make it easy for seniors to live independently or for caregivers to know their charges are safe, but AI also helps us to increase our lifespan. It may even be able to bring us back to life after death. An article in the *Wall Street Journal* discusses whether AI could bestow "digital mortality" on individuals, "preserving the personalities of the departed in virtual form and then allowing them to evolve."[3]

The idea of living forever is appealing to many people and the deployment of AI in this capacity could take off, but would an avatar continue to work? If so, who would get the income? If a person exists in digital form, would grieving family members be able to mourn for them?[4] This, of course, raises more ethical issues on top of the ones we discussed in Chapter Two.

AI can provide seniors with suggestions about food choices and encourage them to build healthy habits, as well as look after the environment. An article by Frontiers in Artificial Intelligence tells us that natural language processing and AI enable food and recipes to be analyzed for their nutritional and sustainability values.[5] Failure to eat nutritious food is considered a major reason why people get diseases, including Covid-19. The article points out how AI can be used to show the link between nutrition and sustainability.

Since so many illnesses are a result of life choices, such as a lack of exercise or eating the wrong food, robots will be able to guide humans to eat properly and stay active. They will also be able to help them recover from trauma. AI can detect cancer, picking up signs and patterns that humans cannot. The use of AI should improve outcomes for people with breast, lung, throat and prostate cancer among others by detecting symptoms early. Therefore, survival rates should increase.

A good example of how AI tools can help with throat cancer is the actor, Val Kilmer.[6] After being diagnosed in 2014, he had an operation which left him unable to speak. His voice was raspy and he had to feed himself through a tube. Working with a software company called Sonantic, he recreated his old speaking voice by feeding hours of recorded audio of himself into an AI algorithm.

AI can help those who have disabilities. Blind people, for instance, can "see" the world around them through the spoken word by using smart glasses that describe their surroundings.[7] Envision has launched smart glasses, powered by AI, that enable users to communicate with others. When faces come into view, the glasses take a picture so they can recognize family and friends. The software understands text and scripts in more than sixty languages, describes images when the user takes a picture, detects colors and reads short pieces of text, such as public transport information.

As robots become more accurate at diagnosing illnesses, they are likely to become more sophisticated. They will get to the stage where they can not only detect illnesses and rectify them, but will suffer from the same illnesses as humans do. For society as a whole and in particular for seniors, who often contract diseases more easily than younger people, the ability of AI to make diagnoses will be good news. In one US study, humans and AI systems were fed information on new patients and were asked to diagnose their medical conditions. For the most part, AI systems beat the humans.[8]

In fact, it will be great for medicine in general. We are already seeing medical practitioners using technology to diagnose disease via video calls. Doctors are able to suggest treatment for a problem without even seeing their patients in person. Instead, they speak with patients via video technologies such as Zoom to identify what is wrong and make a diagnosis.

In the UK, smaller surgeries are tying up with each other to serve a larger community and digitize activity.[9] We believe this will inevitably lead to facial recognition, so people will no longer be able to fool the doctor with a false reading on their condition or pretend to be someone else

Co-author Carole Railton used the healthcare system extensively due to a nasty encounter with Covid. As her case study below shows, technology is changing not only the way medicine is delivered, but also how diseases are diagnosed.

Case study: Healthcare AI in action

Shortly after the pandemic lockdowns came to an end, I (Carole Railton) was in hospital with severe Covid. I had my own room, but one day, I was so fed up with using bedpans that I took the five steps to my bathroom, after having removed all the cables and oxygen to which I was connected.

Just as I was about to use the toilet, a nurse came in and asked—well, to be truthful, screamed at me—what I was doing. Apparently, when you disconnect from the monitors, an alarm goes off at the nurse station. When there are no readings, you are assumed to be dead. Not surprisingly, I was told in no uncertain terms how I was to behave with future toilet requirements. Technology was doing its job.

Since I came out of hospital, technology has continued to keep an eye on me. All my notes are online for my GP to see, along with the X-rays of my lungs that clearly show the blood clots and fluid. Gone are the days when GP surgeries had hand-written notes on patients' health. There's cross fertilization between different departments in hospitals and across medical centers.

I no longer need a prescription to get my medication; it's all done electronically. The pharmacy receives the prescription when it's due and the medication is delivered to me in a timely fashion. The efficiency of this service is beneficial to me and to other seniors.

Technology is helping people age better

Members of the older population are not only taking measures to protect their own health. Some companies are developing products to make aging a better experience for both the older person and the caregiver.

Alzheimer's, a form of dementia, plagues many older people. One UK manufacturer, Chameleon Technology, which supplies smart meters, is working with Liverpool's John Moores University and the local Merseyside NHS Trust to study how technology could help patients living with the disease.[10] It aims to do this by spotting changes in behavior.

Behavioral changes associated with the illness include alterations in routine or abnormal sleep patterns. These abnormalities tend to get more frequent as dementia progresses and can be detected through the energy usage recorded by the smart meter. The data it collects can then be shared with the senior person's family and friends.

Other technologies are being developed to help people with dementia. They include easy-to-read clocks; reminders to take medicines at a certain time; phones that list a contact's picture rather than number; in-home cameras; GPS and tracking devices; and smart appliances such as stoves and ovens that ensure they are switched off.

Playing games can help delay the onset of Alzheimer's disease by keeping the mind alert and active. It can reduce Alzheimer's by up to 50% and AI has a part to play here too.[11] Games on a smartphone or computer are likely to be powered by AI of some sort. Apart from traditional board games like Monopoly and Scrabble, Solitaire or other word games may pop up on your screen, whether on a desktop computer or a cell phone—as the authors have discovered. When you embark on playing one of these games, you are told how old you are—whether you're thirty-five or ninety-five.

Arthritis is a significant problem among the older population and living with the physical challenges it brings usually requires considerable support from others. Once again, AI-powered technology can help. For example, the UK charity Versus Arthritis is using IBM's cognitive technologies in its quest to help people with this condition.[12] To do so, it has introduced an IBM Watson-powered VA to provide personalized support and lifestyle advice. This includes answering questions and fielding answers about arthritis.

IBM says it intends to develop other solutions for the aging population, particularly those with physical and mental disabilities. Its solutions will "incorporate sensors, robotic assistants, the IoT, and other cognitive-powered technologies," all of which will allow clinicians and caregivers to make better care decisions.[13]

In homes, stair lifts are becoming increasingly common, particularly because they are generally easy to use. For the most part, older people can get up and down stairs using a stair lift more easily than they could on their own. Once again, these devices make things easier for caregivers, too.

In 2017, an energy-recycling mechanical staircase was developed to help older people or those who are mobility impaired.[14] Scientist Karen Liu collaborated with other engineers at Georgia Tech and Emory University to produce the prototype of the energy-saving stairs, which do not have to be permanently installed. This device can be placed on existing staircases to make climbing and descending easy on the knees and ankles, but it uses little power.

The mechanical staircase works via a system of springs and pressure sensors. The springs in the stairs compress when someone walks down, "saving energy otherwise dissipated through impact and braking forces at the ankle by 26%."[15] When the person is going up the stairs, the stored energy means there is 37% less impact on the knee than with conventional stairs.

Seniors are becoming more and more active and like to spend time outdoors. Cycling is a favorite pastime and has been increasing in popularity among the older generation worldwide, who can do it alone or with friends. Cycling has significant health benefits, such as increasing the heartrate or relieving stress.

One company that is making the most of this trend is ICEdot, a Tusla, Oklahoma-based crash-sensor maker.[16] If the rider falls off a bike and hits their head on the pavement, a built-in sensor in their cycle helmet will send a signal to the phone of an emergency contact the rider has selected, calling for help. The sensor will also determine the severity of the crash and send the GPS coordinates to the designated emergency contact.

Relationships

The Max Planck Institute, based in Germany, has built robots that gave "soft, warm hugs," which people prefer "over hard, cold hugs."[17] The people involved report feeling trust and affection from the robots, with some even saying they feel understood by them. It is not that they are falling in love with robots, rather that some form of social connection is forming that is often missing from conventional relationships.

It is relatively easy to buy a robot, especially online, whether it's to act as a PA, a sexbot, a companion or simply to do the housework. Even the AI PA on smartphones, such as Siri on an Apple iPhone, could act as a companion.

There are products for couples, some that can be controlled by smartphones or are intended to be used with a tablet, and others that are meant just for individuals, according to an article in *Forbes* magazine.[18] There's even one that can be activated using Alexa no matter where you are in the world,[19] which could put an interesting twist on long-distance relationships.

Intimacy

Since society is changing, with people often being isolated from one another for days and months on end, some are turning to AI-powered robots or "sexbots" for companionship. These robots are usually designed to emulate humans, although critics argue they could easily become objects of unhealthy obsession.

One benefit is that a sexbot can fulfill sexual desires for individuals and couples in a safe way without the risk of sexually transmitted diseases. In some cases, sex toys are connected to apps via IoT technology and sensors, allowing people to control them remotely. Along with some debate over the degree to which sexbots can ease loneliness or give companionship, especially for the bereaved, there are ethical issues, such as privacy, that will have to be considered.

According to YouGovAmerica, surveys taken in 2017 show that 49% of US adults expect that having sex with robots will be commonplace within the next fifty years.[20] The research states that Dr Ian Pearson, a futurist, predicts that by 2050, sex with robots will be more common than human love-making.

However, the Campaign Against Sex Robots is concerned about the capitalism of sexbots and human sexual exploitation.[21] Among its goals is to abolish pornbots in the form of women and girls so that violence and victimization does not occur. The campaign argues that as sexbots become more human, greater inequality in a relationship with a sexbot could occur, but more study is probably required to examine the sex robot/sexual fantasy dynamic and how it could impact seniors. There is concern, however, that developing a relationship with a sexbot could impede alternative networks of affection, whether it be with a person or an animal.

Companionship

In Japan, where the country's birth rate is declining, there are concerns that having sex with robots will make it fall even faster, but this is not a concern for seniors. Older people there have been drawn to a social interaction with a small therapeutic robot called Paro.[22] Paro is an advanced interactive robot, the eighth generation of a design that has been used in Europe and Japan since 2003.

Robotic pets are also becoming increasingly popular as a way to alleviate loneliness. AIST, a Japanese industrial automation company, makes robotic animals that are "cute and cuddly" and a substitute for a real pet. The company says that patients who took part in a study were shown to have increased motor and emotional stimulations. According to the same study, seniors interacting with these robotic pets improve their relationships with other humans and reduce their stress levels.[23]

From a behaviorist's perspective, co-author Carole Railton says of Paro: "We have always had relationships with things that aren't human, so interacting with robots is nothing new. Robots, our new friends, might just be an aid to helping us keep our empathic skills honed so we can use them in times of need."

Violence

Domestic abuse is a global problem and AI has a role to play here, mainly in detecting its likelihood. This problem affects everyone of all ages, including seniors. They may have been impacted by domestic abuse in the past and their children or grandchildren might be impacted currently.

Currently, in the US, roughly one in four women experiences serious intimate partner violence over their lifetime.[24] In England, domestic violence accounts for one-third of all assaults involving injury.[25] It is a problem that cannot be ignored.

In a paper written in February 2020, conventional methods were compared to ML approaches in assessing risk in domestic abuse cases.[26] The paper concluded the following: "Machine-learning methods are far more effective at assessing which victims of domestic violence are most at risk than conventional risk assessments."

It is not just domestic abuse where AI has a role to play in combating violence. City authorities are looking at how it can be best used to reduce the level of violence overall, particularly knife and gun crime and gang issues. While CCTV cameras are commonly used to spot crimes, they can sometimes be misled. People who are hugging may be identified as fighting, although advances in technology and improved behavioral analytics used to power AI have increased its accuracy. Seniors, and every law-abiding citizen, will benefit from this technology at a societal level.

Summary

In this chapter, we have taken a close look at the benefits of AI to our healthcare and safety as we get older. We have covered:

- How AI can empower seniors to stay healthy

- The possibility of immortality

- How AI can help in the diagnosis of diseases such as cancer and Alzheimer's

- The part AI can play in combating loneliness

- How AI can make our city streets safer places for everyone

AI is still an emerging technology so there is a long way to go and plenty of research to be done. We also need to ensure that ethical discussions are ongoing so that AI doesn't end up doing more harm than good.

In the next chapter, we will look at the subject of wealth in relation to technology.

5

Technology
And Wealth

Technology plays a crucial role in the financial services sector, which has embraced it enthusiastically. This industry is adopting a range of AI and ML tools with the aim of ensuring that the customer has a fulfilling experience in their interaction with banking and wealth management services and feels secure in the transactions they are carrying out. However, with nearly all interactions between customers and financial services companies being online, many seniors are simply expected to "get used to it."

With the rapid growth in the older population, financial services packages that meet the needs of seniors are becoming increasingly important. Companies will have to do more to cater for seniors, not only to prevent fraud, but also to stop financial exploitation. In the future, these companies will have to ensure their offerings are geared to the needs of older individuals, allowing such individuals to be independent and self-reliant.

To cater for seniors, the issues with which financial services companies will have to deal are numerous. They include facilitating powers of attorney and options to help carers have access to a senior's money: issues that don't tend to affect the younger generations.

AI has been integrated into banking, insurance, trading and investment services. AI-powered tools not only enable firms to be competitive, but they allow them to assess credit quality, price and market insurance contracts, automate client interactions and optimize trading. AI tools can also help financial institutions with optimizing scarce capital, back-testing models, analyzing the market impact of trading large positions, and with compliance, surveillance, data quality assessment and fraud detection.

This chapter will look at how seniors can achieve, preserve and increase their wealth. It will discuss not only how seniors interact with financial service companies and how technology can help with this interaction, but how making the most of technology can help seniors in their investments and trading on the stock market. It will also examine how essential it is for seniors to know their way around technology if they want to secure a job or become an entrepreneur.

Online banking

Banks are increasingly using AI apps to collect and analyze data, making it easier for them to review millions of transactions. Forecasts suggest that banks in the US could save nearly US$447 billion by 2023 if they implement AI applications.[1] As more bank branches close as a result of advancements in technology, seniors who have been reluctant to embrace online banking will have to do so to ensure they have access to their money.

For older customers venturing into online banking for the first time, fraud is a big concern. They often react to the idea of carrying out any financial transactions online with horror and fear; they believe that any information they give to a bank in this way could be stolen by an unscrupulous third party, but in reality, they have no need to fear online banking. As a result of using AI tools, banks have become excellent at detecting unusual transactions and often don't allow such transfers to take place until the customer has confirmed they are genuine. People can also set a daily spending limit online to help them manage their finances and live to a budget.

Seniors who prefer to make deposits and withdrawals at a bank branch or write a check rather than using online banking are going to have to learn to adapt. Some banks have even stopped issuing or accepting checks, preferring instead to interact with their customers via their computer, cell phones or tablet. In the UK, the financial ombudsman is considering paperless banking within the next ten years.[2] In New Zealand it has already happened. Banks there no longer issue checks at all.[3]

As the online banking model becomes ever more successful and bank branches are closing, seniors will have no choice but to bank online. Co-author Lucia's late mother was reluctant to embrace online banking. She had always gone into a bank branch and didn't like the idea of using any technology. In contrast, her late father embraced online banking with alacrity and always checked his investments—principally stocks—online. For many, especially the less mobile, online banking is a good thing. Not having to go into a bank does have its pluses.

Dennis Reed, director of Silver Voices, which campaigns for the over-sixties, fears millions of older people will be cut adrift from the financial system.[4] This comes after a warning that cash could be phased out eventually. Reed said:

> "We would seek reassurance from the new government that they are going to treat this seriously because so many people still rely on cash… Maybe thirty or forty years down the road we may be able to talk about this again, but at the moment it's not possible for people to be disenfranchised in this way."

One huge advantage of AI is that it has made it possible for seniors to get served more quickly than they would in a bank. The use of voice recognition technology can determine how old someone is and push them up the line accordingly when they're waiting for bank interaction. Nuance Communications Inc., an American firm, is already deploying technology to do this. According to its website, it has developed an age-detection AI app called Nuance Gatekeeper that can single out senior citizens for priority service.[5] It can identify users from the way they talk, tap and text, and determine if the caller is a child, adult or senior. Even though this technology doesn't require complicated pins and passwords to access an account—another bonus—it can help to prevent fraud by using biometric verification, using voice and behavior, and AI fraud prevention technology.[6]

Why did Nuance Communications Inc. deploy AI technology? It wanted age-recognition tools to address a spike in customer service calls during the coronavirus pandemic, when seniors became more susceptible to fraud more than ever, probably because they also needed immediate service. Nuance's first customer was the Spanish telecom giant Telefónica, which has 344 million customers over fourteen countries.[7]

The algorithms in Nuance's tools can detect age easily and "enable more effective and efficient customer protection and service," explained Brett Beranek, who is responsible for overseeing security at Nuance, in a press release.[8] Beranek says Nuance's AI is accurate because it detects more than 1,000 micro-characteristics that the human ear can't process or comprehend. Speaking to *Fast Company* magazine, though, he wasn't forthcoming on margins of error.[9] He merely said that as speakers approach sixty, the algorithm gets less accurate. This inaccuracy reaches double digits for customers between the ages of sixty and sixty-five and it's down to Nuance's users to decide the acceptable level of inaccuracy based on how the technology is to be used.

As with other AI technologies, it's possible for age detection to be abused, but Beranek is aware of the risks. For this reason, Nuance's technology isn't available to everyone, including repressive regimes, nor does it support large-scale public surveillance.

To explain to seniors how they can use online banking safely, Age UK, a charity that addresses the needs of older people, has put a checklist for online banking on its website.[10] This explains how to set up online banking, access the bank's smartphone app, receive bank statements and keep money and one's identity safe. Age UK also highlights how bank websites are encrypted, how and why websites and apps have timed logout, why multiple steps are required to log in, why an e-reader might be chosen and how the details to whom money is transferred can be double-checked.[11]

With access to banking facilities getting more difficult for an aging population as bank branches close across the world, Age UK argues that banks must guarantee access to money for everyone. It has looked at age-friendly banking with the American Association of Retired Persons (AARP), a US organization with a membership of nearly 38 million, dedicated to the needs and interests of adults who are over fifty. Together, they have written a report entitled "Age friendly banking" that looks at "products and facilities that remain accessible and easy to use as people age, assist caregivers and prevent financial exploitation" and why banks offer these services.[12]

The report states that it is important for banks to become age-friendly for several reasons:

- To adapt to the needs of an aging society

- To deliver a better service to existing and new customers and improve customer satisfaction

- To build a reputation for age-friendly service that may give competitive advantage

- To develop systems and products that better suit all customers, regardless of age

- To reduce fraud and financial exploitation

- To improve the relationship between the bank and its stakeholders

- To help rebuild the reputation of the banking sector following the crash of 2008

- To meet obligations under equality and human rights legislation

Banks and the metaverse

Over the past few years, banks have become more like financial technology (fintech) companies, which use technology to change the delivery of financial services products and, hopefully, make them more efficient. Banks and other fintech companies are increasingly moving into the metaverse.

The growth of the metaverse is likely to be one of the main global trends in future years. For seniors who want to interact with someone at a bank branch, the metaverse should help. There is also greater use of chatbots by banks. Some banks, like KB Kookmin in South Korea, are already offering individualized consultations in the metaverse.[13]

By using AI tools, banks will be able to execute e-payments more efficiently and easily so they can compete with the money transfer companies that specialize in that area. In that respect, banks may become retailers with customers able to choose products in the metaverse and pay for them immediately.

History

A little bit of history may help explain why seniors have to get accustomed to online banking. In the 1990s, banks needed to cut costs. Moving to an online model was the best way to do this, but many were reluctant to make the move. There was much debate over the pros and cons of online banking and the need for bank branches, known as "bricks and mortar."

Wells Fargo, a US bank, was one of the first banks in the world to offer internet banking back in 1995, alongside Citibank, Chemical and Chase.[14] Although banks in the UK introduced internet banking, the first bank in the UK to have an internet-only agenda was Egg, the banking arm of Prudential Plc, the insurance company. Egg was launched in October 1998 (in fact Lucia was an early customer of this bank) and it offered savings, general insurance, loans, credit cards and mortgage products. It offered its first online credit card in September 1999.[15]

Since then, all banks across the world have internet and telephone banking, from the UK to NZ, so it is now possible to carry out internet banking in the UK while you are in NZ, and vice versa. Passwords, which are becoming increasingly sophisticated, are always used.

Investing and trading

Some seniors may have disposable income that they choose to invest in the stock market. This can now be done electronically. AI technology has not only helped to ensure better outcomes with trading, but it has improved the entire customer experience. However, it takes time to become accustomed to what AI tools have to offer.

Until now, decision-making in trading has been largely dependent on human knowledge, but this is changing. According to a study by UK research firm Coalition, electronic trades accounted for almost 45% of revenues in cash equities trading in 2019.[16] Hedge funds also use AI tools to get investment ideas and build portfolios.

AI technology makes it possible to dispose of multiple trades simultaneously, which is particularly useful if someone is day trading. Robo-advisers can analyze data points and execute trades, ensuring trading is more accurate and efficient, and less risky.

When it comes to selecting the stocks in which to invest, AI technology takes out the emotion from the decision-making process. Some seniors may like to invest in companies that are developing products for their age group, where AI may be used to make existing operations more powerful, perhaps by developing robotics, self-driving cars or VAs, helping with content creation, product recommendations or healthcare.

Maintaining income through work

It is increasingly common for people over sixty to continue to work. It may be they have no choice, wish to continue to earn money, like the social aspect of working or want to keep their minds and/or bodies active. All of these and more are valid reasons for seniors wanting to remain in the workforce. Unfortunately, there is a great deal of frustration among older people that job hunting is proving to be difficult. Many say that ageism is at play.

Ageism and discrimination

In interviews conducted during the research for this book, one senior in a New Zealand care facility told us, "Employers want somebody in their twenties with twenty years of experience."

Another retired person commented, "It is quite difficult to enter the workforce once you have left it at an advanced age. The world moves on so fast and all the technology is well beyond me."[17]

Even though ageism clearly exists, older people can be proactive when job hunting. Sometimes the fact that you are older makes employers believe that using new technology will be beyond you, so it is important you not only speak the language of technology, but understand it. If you fail to do so, getting back into the labor market (especially if you are female) can be tough.

An older person's reluctance to use technology has been likened to them not embracing a rebrand of a favorite product. When co-author Carole Railton was doing some branding work in Nigeria, one of the products she looked at was a beer marketed to the older population for health purposes. Carole took it out of bottles and put it in tin cans, which made the beer cheaper to transport and more acceptable to the younger population, but the older people didn't buy it any longer. Although the company was pleased, increasing its turnover and profit, seniors stopped drinking its product as a result of the rebrand.

Seniors need to be up to speed with how the job market works now as compared to how it was when they first entered employment. They need to be aware of how different industries are evolving, perhaps using social media such as LinkedIn to maintain industry networks. A social-media presence shows that seniors are up to date with technology.

Undoubtedly, some older people find learning to use the latest technology easier than others. Sometimes it is because they have been on courses or grown up with technology, even though their experiences will likely be somewhat out of date. Some have simply developed a rapport with technology.

Case study: A biased view

Even if you speak the language of the latest technology and understand it, the biased perception remains in the minds of some people that you do not know how to use it if you are a senior. This is, of course, wrong.

This problem was highlighted by comments made to Lucia when she was teaching in Vietnam. Some teachers (all of whom were younger than her) assumed that she would find the technology—in this case an electronic whiteboard—difficult to use because she was "too old." The fact that many of the younger teachers weren't competent with that technology was beside the point.

What this showed Lucia is that people's perception of who is competent with technology and who is not can hold seniors back. It can prevent opportunities coming their way or cause them to be reluctant to take up new opportunities, or both. This must change. Although it is for society to address this, some nations, like Vietnam, are less willing to address the issue of seniors than others, like the UK, US and NZ. Arguably, however, there is some way to go.

Anecdotes from friends and family who are older and have had difficulty getting job interviews suggest that employers are often reluctant to employ older people. Even those over forty find it hard to secure interviews. A survey undertaken in 2002 by Massey University in New Zealand for the Ministry of Social Development showed that employers have positive views of older workers when it comes to "reliability, loyalty and job commitment."[18] However, older workers are associated negatively with resistance to using technology and change, being less flexible and less willing to work long hours. Seniors are also seen as less willing to be trained and become team players. This leads to missed opportunities for seniors to enhance their skills and share their experiences.

More recently, the UN released a report "Ageism is a global challenge."[19] It maintains that people over fifty live more isolated and unhappy lives. The report calls for "urgent action to combat ageism and better measurement and reporting to expose ageism for what it is—an insidious scourge on society." It says that the Covid-19 pandemic showed how widespread ageism is and points out that in some instances, "age has been used as the sole criterion for access to medical care, lifesaving therapies and for physical isolation."

Employers and governments can do something about ageism. For example, working arrangements need to be more flexible. There also need to be more public awareness campaigns and perhaps financial incentives for employers who hire older workers.

The future of work

What do developments in technology, and AI specifically, mean for older workers? Will they be forced into low-wage service jobs, or will they get the training they need to adapt to an economy that increasingly demands high-tech skills?

There are many scare stories on the future of work. Most suggest that as new technologies emerge, especially AI, this could be the end of some jobs. On the flip side, new ones will emerge. Linda P. Fried, Dean of the Mailman School of Public Health at Columbia University, says:

"In many cases, it [AI] will eliminate the need for jobs in areas of expertise people built over their careers and transform those jobs into things that weren't previously imagined."[20]

Thomas Malone, a professor at MIT's Sloan School of Management, speaking at the Mailman School of Public Health at Columbia University in January 2018, is more optimistic.[21] He said that "throughout human history, major technological advances, like the invention of the printing press, have created more jobs than they destroyed. AI could be a positive for older workers by serving as a 'cognitive prosthesis' to compensate for age-related memory loss."

Seniors should be part of the labor market as studies have shown that working into our sixties and seventies is good for the health,[22] but several issues need to be resolved. Will this mean an old workforce? Will discrimination be overcome? If discrimination comes into play when employers are recruiting, society will not benefit from the wisdom, knowledge and experience that older people can offer.

Summary

In this chapter, we have looked at the impact technology has on how we manage our financial affairs. We have also discussed the relevance of older people to the workforce. The topics we have explored include:

- Online banking

- Technology's part in investing and trading

- Working in later life

- Age discrimination when it comes to the employment market

Technology plays a crucial role in the financial services sector, which is adopting a range of AI and ML tools. With the rapid growth in the older population, financial services firms will have to do more to cater for seniors. Employers also need to overcome any bias they may have related to age as seniors continue to bring valuable skills to the employment market. On the other hand, seniors need to make sure their skills are up to date, particularly where technology is concerned, so they are attractive to potential employers.

6

Technology And Day-to-day Living

Technology, and AI in particular, has made it easy for seniors to live more comfortably than ever before. They can use it to read, shop, search for information and carry out everyday chores such as cooking and cleaning. Moreover, AI has ensured that these things are done securely.

This chapter will look at some of the ways that seniors can benefit from the use of technology in their daily lives.

Reading and dyslexia

Deteriorating eyesight is something that many seniors have to live with. For this reason, they tend to prefer an e-reader, such as a Kindle or a Kobo, rather than a paperback or hard-cover book. E-readers can be especially useful for older people since they allow them to enlarge the print.

The first versions of e-readers did not use AI, but this is changing. For example, Booklyn.co is an e-reader whose signature feature is an AI bot.[1] This allows readers to ask questions about a page of any site-supported book in English, of which there are several million, and view answers in real time. There is also a dictionary search that has bookmarking, annotating features and shareable quotations.

This e-reader helps with speed reading and the learning of new languages. It has a microphone, for example, that allows users to read the words out loud, while a translation appears on their screen. Language learners can highlight or double click on words so that they get an accurate translation and the audio will play the correct pronunciation. Translations are available in English, Spanish, Portuguese, Italian, German, Polish and French, and there are plans to expand on these.[2] There are also plans to develop the AI bot further to include book summarization, an advanced search feature, the opportunity to learn sophisticated language and grammar points, and a digital PA.

Case study: Technology and dyslexia

Technology is being used to help dyslexics. Co-author Carole Railton has suffered from dyslexia throughout her life and credits technology with making things easier for her. This is what she has to say on the subject.

"I never read a book from cover to cover until I was forty-five and got glasses. It was not until then that I found out I was dyslexic. I hope what has happened to me is true for all seniors with dyslexia: that your reading, spelling and concentration will improve, and much of it is thanks to technology.

"New technology and AI are useful for dyslexics since AI chooses the right words when you are typing. It understands sentence formation, words that naturally fit with what you're writing, which is a great help.

"In the old days, when typing on my computer, I would just get a choice of words that began with the letter I had typed. This made it impossible for me to choose the word that was appropriate as I had no idea how to spell, so I would not recognize the right one. This could, of course, create terrible problems in business, especially without the benefit of a PA who could choose the right words. Voice recognition worked up to a point, but if there was an incorrect word in a sentence, I would not be able to see it.

"Automatic correction is another useful tool, for long and short writings. I type the first few letters, and then AI suggests words, including tenses of verbs. Even more importantly for dyslexics, we can talk to a computer and it types what we are saying. This saves time, is convenient and is certainly less stressful than trying to write.

"At school, I spent my time in a low-level class, being told I did not try hard enough. No one cared that I couldn't read. Instead, the teachers used to bring me women's magazines to look at rather than investigating why I wasn't progressing. Luckily, I excelled at sport and was in all the sports teams. I was also quite good at art, otherwise my confidence would have taken a huge hit.

"Dyslexics cannot learn parrot fashion and most have a poor short-term memory. These issues can make it hard for them to learn math tables, languages or lines in a book or play. You will not find many dyslexic actors, but there are many in the visual professions such as photography and graphic design. Despite dyslexia, my career has been

> successful. Since I was unable to read, when I became a
> manager, I made sure I had a PA.
>
> "As I have gotten older, my dyslexia has lessened, thank
> goodness. Wearing colored glasses, which can alleviate
> visual distortions, has greatly improved my reading ability
> and with the help of technology, I have had two books
> published. For me, new technology has been a godsend.
> It saves me an amazing amount of time."

Dyslexia is a learning difficulty that affects reading and writing, but not intelligence. It afflicts about 10% of the UK population, according to the British Dyslexia Association (2018).[3] Of this figure, about 4%, or 7.3 million people, are at the extreme end of the dyslexia spectrum, but this figure is thought to be an underestimate. According to Dyslexia Action (2017), it is more likely to be around 16% of the population, or 11.5 million people.[4]

Globally, the same source suggests that between 5% and 10% of the population experiences dyslexia, which equates to around 700 million people worldwide, but this figure too is likely to be an underestimate. Some evidence suggests that the figure is around 17% of the world's population.[5] Successful dyslexics, many of whom have helped to change the world, include Leonardo Da Vinci, Bill Gates, Richard Branson, Walt Disney, Albert Einstein, Orlando Bloom, Whoopi Goldberg and Keira Knightley.[6]

Travel

Travel is another area where seniors can benefit from AI. They are often retired, so have the time—and potentially the money— to go see the world. The travel sector uses technology, usually AI, extensively to make the experience smooth and easy. Technology can enable travelers to book and pay for tickets online, check in for flights online, use an airline kiosk where the tickets and bag tag are printed, send their luggage through the weighing belt, use facial recognition at airports, and book accommodation.

Websites such as Kayak, booking.com, viator.com, Trivago, Expedia or Webjet use AI and natural language processing to ensure customers find their answers quickly and easily without calling the help desk or sending an email. When it comes to accommodation websites, AI ensures that pricing differs according to demand. This is known as dynamic pricing.

Some seniors still prefer to use travel agents because they do not feel technologically savvy. What will they do in a post-pandemic era of online form filling as countries endeavor to keep all variants of Covid out if they do not have a computer, tablet or smartphone?

Hotels

A new senior hotel experience is being trialed in Europe, according to Swiss-based hotelier, Michael Butler, speaking exclusively with co-author Lucia Dore in 2021. People will be able to seek medical and nutritional advice via the TV, for example, and it will be possible for them to speak with a GP. This recognizes that people in different decades want and need different things when they're away from home.

Seniors can also benefit from the fact that more hotels are using AI to make the customer experience engaging for them and give them a wide variety of choice. As well as being used to improve the guest experience, AI can aid revenue management and automate daily operations. In the dining room, robots may even serve diners.

Hotels such as the Radisson Blu Edwardian in London and Manchester use AI concierges to check guests in or out, deliver room service and answer questions 24/7. "Edward," a VA, is already available at about twelve Radisson Blu locations.[7] It can receive guest complaints via SMS, report on hotel amenities, and give directions and tips. Although Edward can't necessarily bring what the guest requests itself, such as more towels or toothpaste, it can liaise with someone who can.

AI can also be used for environmental and social impact reporting, as is demonstrated by Hilton's "LightStay," a system designed to track its hotels' environmental performance.[8] It was launched in 2009.

Accessibility of transport

Access to transport is a key issue faced by seniors, who may be dealing with declining eyesight, hearing, mobility and/or reflexes. Many companies are developing AI-inspired solutions, giving seniors greater independence outside their homes.

For example, Olli the driverless bus that we met in Chapter One entered service in the Municipality of Reggio Emilia in Italy in 2021.[9] A project that develops autonomous carbon-neutral vehicles is Masdar City of Abu Dhabi. It was started in 2006 by Mubadala Investment Company and is attracting partners from all over the world that want to develop new transport solutions.[10] Masdar City aims to be an incubator for AI innovation and a growing number of AI specialist companies are joining it. It even has a University of AI.[11]

Shopping

AI is reinventing the retail landscape. Seniors can benefit from a wide range of AI-powered services, from computer vision—that is technology that allows computers and systems to derive information from digital images, videos and other visual inputs—to customized promotions in real time. Seniors do not even have to leave their home if they want to go shopping; they can talk to friendly bots or humans and get things delivered, probably within a few days of ordering them, if not sooner.

Amazon's "Just Walk Out" retail outlet represents how we are likely to see shops operate in the future.[12] This will make shopping easier for seniors, who will not have to remember to bring any credit cards or cash with them when they leave their homes; the outlet uses technology that automatically detects when products are taken from or returned to the shelves and keeps track of them in a virtual basket. When customers have finished shopping, they just leave the store, their Amazon account is charged and a receipt is sent by email. At the area's local sports shop, the customer only has to put the items into a basket where they are added up without even removing the items from the basket. The bill prints out, you tap and load the items into your shopping bag. Job done!

Seniors can also benefit from shopping online. The global lockdowns during the Covid-19 pandemic helped online shopping to take off in a big way, although it was gaining in popularity prior to 2020. Sites like Amazon are easy to use, and delivery and returns are usually processed speedily. When a friend returned a faulty vacuum cleaner to Amazon, another was delivered before the company had received the return. All that she had to do was print out a label emailed to her by Amazon, take the label and vacuum cleaner to a local store and it was done. No one even queried why she was returning it.

The fashion industry

The deployment of AI in the fashion industry will make it easy for seniors to come to decisions about what to buy and what to wear. AR and VR will enhance the buying experience online, this technology allowing customers to see themselves in a garment in front of a mirror/screen without physically having to go into a shop.

AI helps brands forecast fashion trends, colors and fabrics, and design their products accordingly. This will help to cut wastage, which is great news for the environment. Digital fitting room solution Truefit uses personal shopper data to help customers find the perfect fit for apparel and shoes.[13] The Japanese-owned company Virtusize enables retailers to build brand loyalty using virtual sizing tools to increase customer satisfaction and the number of repeat purchases, and reduce returns.[14]

Virtual models not only allow designers to show their latest creations worldwide (even when large fashion shows were prohibited due to Covid restrictions), they also help reduce waste by showcasing clothes that haven't actually been manufactured. Shudu Gram, a computer-generated social-media personality, is considered to be the world's first digital supermodel.[15] Other computer-generated models have joined Shudu Gram as virtual influencers with thousands of followers on social media. These include Lil Miquela, Lightning and Noonouri.[16]

Seniors will be able to buy well-known brands like Gucci, Prada and Balenciaga on virtual platforms too. Gemma Sheppard, a stylist on the UK's *10 Years Younger* TV program, became the first stylist to enter the Facebook universe.[17] She charges clients real money to dress models.

Several companies are using technology to make fashion more eco-friendly and sustainable—something that an increasing number of seniors are becoming passionate about. A more environmentally friendly and sustainable world means our surroundings are likely to improve—and our food, too. Historically, fashion has been one of the world's most polluting industries.

Smart clothes

Smart or high-tech clothing, which could be socks, shoes, sleepwear, casual or active wear, is becoming increasingly popular. It not only makes life easy, but can alert the wearer to injuries. Seniors who take part in sport will certainly benefit from the sensors built into smart clothing to help in decision-making in the case of an injury. Tracking allows caregivers and relatives to ensure that seniors are safe at all times.[18]

The technology in smart clothing can identify, analyze and potentially prevent health issues from arising via circuity woven into the fabrics. This is known as "adaptive" clothing and is expected to benefit those who wear them by, for example, being able to dress more easily.[19] Manufacturers such as Tommy Hilfiger and Ralph Lauren are among the companies experimenting with smart technology. Tommy Hilfiger is experimenting with technology that tracks and rewards users for the number of purchases they make.[20] Hoodies, jeans and jackets may be fitted with these tracking devices.

Smart homes

Seniors, and perhaps their caregivers, can only benefit from the arrival of the smart home. A smart home means that devices such as refrigerators, washing machines, air conditioners, heaters, ovens and entertainment systems are monitored and/or controlled.

One example of AI technology being used in homes, particularly in retirement villages, is convection stove tops that alert the user when the element is too hot to touch or a saucepan spills over. Elements also switch off automatically when they are not being used. For obvious reasons, these are becoming increasingly popular with seniors.

Ovens too have become more sophisticated, allowing people to cook in a number of different ways. Self-cleaning has become the norm. Refrigerators can alert the user or caregiver to the fact that the door has been left open. Seniors can opt to switch on the lights or the heating at home when they are out and about, all made possible because of AI technology.

Media and entertainment

AI is transforming the media and entertainment business, impacting on everything from content creation to the consumer experience. When it comes to the media, seniors can choose which programs to watch and play them back when it suits. The fact that programs can be recorded and played at any time is a simple example of AI. The availability of on demand services impacts how everyone, including seniors, choose which media to follow and television programs to watch. There is also radio on demand.

Newsrooms are being transformed because of AI, particularly in the realm of content creation, but it is not only traditional media that is benefiting. Email and social media are as well. How often have you been checking emails and been asked whether you want to unsubscribe from an online publication because you haven't opened any messages from the company for some time?

When you're browsing social media, ads often pop up about the exact things that you have been looking at online. This kind of tailoring of ads happens because your online presence is being monitored using AI. An AI-powered monitoring and listening tool tracks a brand's social-media profiles so its audience can be targeted.

Technology expressly for seniors

Seniors may sometimes find that the technology they are using is not designed with them in mind. The anxiety that this engenders can manifest itself in fear and a lack of confidence in using technology in general, but thankfully, this is changing. New devices are being designed with seniors in mind.

One company that has done just this is GrandPad.[21] The founder designed a tablet so his eighty-year-old mother could use it with ease, but it has proven so successful that several organizations and associations are encouraging people who are seventy-five or over to benefit from it. Some associations are even making GrandPad available to lease.

The GrandPad tablet rests on a wireless charging cradle with a long power cable. It has a simple interface and a larger screen than a cell phone. It can be used as a phone, for emails and for video calls, and acts as a digital photo frame when it's not in use. It supports its own video-calling app as well as a dedicated Zoom app. For the hearing impaired, messages can be typed and they appear on screen during a call. A GrandPad can replace a cell phone because it's portable and seniors can take it with them when they go out.

GrandPad does not require wifi and comes with 4G LTE configured and ready to go. Unlike an iPad or tablet, GrandPad has no pop-up alerts. Seniors are protected from online scams because there is an encrypted private network of approved contacts uploaded by a family member so it is not possible to connect with another person of a group that has not already been vetted and approved. Joining any group is by invitation only. This is because communications between the tablet and the internet are encrypted, and no phone numbers or email addresses are viewable.

Software updates and pop-ups that appear on regular phones and tablets and can confuse seniors are removed from the GrandPad, which keeps itself up to date. This is great for reducing the stress and fear some seniors feel about using technology.

Seniors, like most people, have benefited from the growth of video calls, whether they be via Zoom, Skype, Google Meet or any other technology. This technology has helped to reduce social isolation, allowing seniors to stay in touch with their children, grandchildren and friends from the comfort of their own homes. According to research, prolonged isolation for a senior has a detrimental effect on their health that is the equivalent to smoking fifteen cigarettes a day.[22]

Summary

This chapter has looked at some of the ways in which seniors can benefit from the use of technology in their day-to-day lives, including:

- Reading aids

- How technology can help people with dyslexia

- Travel and transport

- Shopping

- Choosing clothing

- Smart homes

We have also looked at the increase in technology designed expressly with seniors in mind. This can only be good news and should go a long way to overcoming the fear we may feel when confronted with something new and unknown, like the latest AI-powered device.

PART THREE
THE FUTURE OF SENIORS

Many older people dislike technology—some even hate it. They tend to say that they have lived without technology for so long, there is no need for them to use it now. Certainly, they assert, they have no reason to rely on technology as younger people do now.

By refusing to learn about new technologies or use new gadgets, whether they be computers or smartphones, are seniors not losing out? How can seniors be encouraged to use technology? These are just two of the questions that will be answered in this last part of the book.

Part Three will also explore how seniors can engage with technology and influence future developments. We'll look at how seniors interact with technology and how this impacts their body language. Some of the discussion is around the importance of design to ensure that seniors engage more with technology. Does design matter? How can it be improved? What role can seniors play in deciding which design is best for them?

7

Ways Technology Can Enhance The Life Of Seniors

A lack of understanding of technology—AI in particular—and its benefits, as well as difficulty in using a particular technology, such as a smartphone or computer, means that many seniors are reluctant to migrate from the old to the new. This is a mistake.

The challenge society must address is the lack of confidence some older people feel about using technology. We must find ways to boost the skill sets of seniors so that they enter the later years of their lives in the modern world with enthusiasm. Remember, everyone gets old.

Seniors themselves must consider whether they want to embrace new technology, much of it based on AI, or let the benefits pass them by. Technology, often in the form of social media, has enabled seniors to meet new friends, keep in touch with old ones and learn new skills.

In all probability, the stark truth is that seniors have less time left to live than the younger generations. Surely, then, it makes sense for them to adopt systems that make their lives as easy as possible. What is the best way to give seniors the tools they need to learn about AI? Would understanding the benefits of AI encourage seniors to embrace technology?

This chapter will answer these questions, examining how seniors can be encouraged to engage with technology. It will look at what seniors want from technology and how they could benefit from embracing it, which is highlighted in the case study at the end of the chapter.

Chapter Seven will also explore online courses and the training of seniors to use and understand technology. Making training available to seniors is a must if society is to benefit from their wisdom and knowledge, as well as enabling them to re-enter the workforce and live healthy lives.

What do seniors want from technology?

The reasons why some seniors adopt new technology are likely to be twofold: they're compelled to do so and they want to make their lives easier. These reasons are important for anyone who realizes seniors need to be convinced to engage with technology to consider. Using technology is the best thing for us all to do, yet some seniors still insist, "I have managed before without technology. Why do I have to use it now?"

Necessity can compel seniors to use technology. A good example is the Covid-19 pandemic, which increased social isolation and, as a result, technology adoption. Some 44% of people aged fifty and older are more comfortable with technology now than they were before the pandemic, according to a 2021 World Economic Forum report.[1]

A study carried out by AARP in April 2021 reinforces this.[2] It shows that the pandemic led to seniors feeling more confident using technology, including email, social media, video calling friends and relatives, thereby avoiding social isolation. A study from December 2021 shows that more than 80% of people aged fifty-plus, 79% of those in their sixties and 72% of those in their seventies rely on technology to stay connected.[3]

Sometimes, it's something as simple as a Christmas present that compels a senior to change their habits. When a loved one gives them a technological device, seniors often make sure they use it, even if it's something they have previously been reluctant to adopt. For example, they may have been resistant to buying a smartphone, but if they receive one as a Christmas gift, they are highly likely to use it.

Seniors are also more likely to embrace technology if it makes their way of life comfortable, helps them achieve a better standard of living than they have currently and means they can remain independent. This is highlighted by the case study at the end of this chapter.

Seniors often become frustrated with technology. "It's not working," is a refrain co-author Lucia heard many times from her late father, especially when it came to his cell phone—and he used technology well, for the most part. Often, the problem was that he was unable to use the small keypad on his phone or read the letter size of the words in text messages he received.

Since some seniors are not comfortable and confident using technology, a device being designed to enhance rather than detract from the health and wellbeing of these seniors when they use it is important. This was highlighted by WHO in a global report on ageism published in February 2022.[4] In it, Alana Officer, unit head of Demographic Change and Healthy Ageing at WHO, says: "To ensure that AI technologies play a beneficial role, ageism must be identified and eliminated from their design, development, use and evaluation."

The problems associated with technology design and seniors have gone back decades. Seniors tend to want web pages to be simple and clear, and navigation to be easy. One study from 2005 shows that many seniors like a website to be user-friendly with a simple interface.[5] "A simpler and more uniformly designed internet would help to break down the psychological barriers outlined," it states. Even though that study was carried out some time ago, this problem with web design still stands.

Web pages for older people—in fact, for everyone—must be easy to navigate, the design familiar and pleasant to look at and the words easy to read. These pages must also be responsive and provide all the information that seniors (and others) are looking for. For this reason, websites need to be comprehensive, informative and up to date.

Is online help user-friendly? Is it easy to access? Do only chatbots reply to online enquiries or does a real person do it? Is there a telephone advice center? Would seniors (and those with disabilities) benefit from a simplification of online help and error message terminology?

Jobs will not be taken over by robots

If seniors are to embrace technology, some need to be convinced that it is the right thing to do. Take robots, for example. Many seniors are encouraged to use them for companionship, as a PA or for the distribution of medication, but they worry that to do so means that robots will take over the jobs of the younger generation. Even if robots do this, new jobs will be created in their place.

A Pew Research survey found that "Americans are roughly twice as likely to express worry (72%) than enthusiasm (33%) about a future in which robots and computers are capable of doing many jobs that are currently done by humans."[6] There are scare stories on the future of work. Yes, as new technologies emerge, especially AI, some types of jobs could come to an end, but at the same time, new ones will emerge. Technology is likely to create jobs and opportunities we haven't even thought about yet.

In a special report entitled "Automation and anxiety," journalist Tom Standage looks at history to explain the impact of technological developments on the workforce.[7] He says that although machines caused temporary effects on the rate of unemployment, which rose immediately after the Industrial Revolution, the formation of the working class and the proletariat led to an entirely new form of employment. The Industrial Revolution caused more tasks to be automated, which prompted workers to focus on tasks that machines could not do, introducing an explosive growth in output and drastically increasing employment in other sectors.

Over the years, technology has enabled tasks to be performed more quickly, cheaply and efficiently. The introduction of automatic teller machines (ATMs) by banks is an example, with the first ATM being introduced in September 1969 in the USA.[8] ATMs made the running of banks less costly, so more branches were opened up, stimulating an increase in bank teller employment.

Upgrading skills

One of the best ways to feel confident about new technology, especially if you are planning to re-enter the workforce, is to gain the skills you need to use it. To do this, maybe you can join a computer class, for example. Some are online (which presupposes that you have some computer skills to start with) and others are a hybrid of offline and online teaching.

What is the best way for teaching to take place? Is a classroom environment best? Would you prefer to be taught by a stranger or someone you know? Following many discussions with people who teach classes to seniors, we (the authors) are firmly convinced that seniors learn more effectively if they are taught by a family member, rather than by someone outside the family or in a classroom environment.

That said, learning in a classroom sometimes works. Co-author Lucia's late father attended a computer course when he was in his seventies where he learned all about using a keyboard, emails and storing photographs. He found it very useful, although he was reluctant to use anything other than a Dell PC, since he had learned on that. Attending a computer course certainly enabled him to use his computer and smartphone better. Unfortunately, Lucia's late mother would never touch a computer and found using a smartphone difficult as a result.

You can find a list of courses available in the "Help and support" page. The question this learning raises is whether IT courses should be rolled out in rest homes and/or retirement villages. Is this something that communities and policy makers should consider? Moreover, should these courses be available to everyone who wants to join one? For those older people who want to re-enter the workforce, maybe employers should offer training courses and career advice.

The International Labor Organization (ILO) certainly thinks so.[9] It argues that public employment services should offer training opportunities and career guidance tailored to the needs of older workers. Arguably, all employers should offer paid training courses to their employees, especially when it comes to technology, but empirical evidence suggests that employers, and older workers too, may see training and professional development as more relevant for younger people.[10] This can lead to missed opportunities for seniors to enhance their skills and share their experiences.

Understanding technology

A major reason why many employers are reluctant to consider recruiting older people is the perception that seniors do not understand technology. It certainly helps if a senior speaks the language of the latest technology, as we discussed in Chapter Five. It is even better if they understand it. This can make it much easier for them to access the job market.

The population is aging, as the ILO points out.[11] Its 2020 report shows that the proportion of people aged fifty-five and over will increase significantly in all regions of the world over the coming decades. By 2050, more than three-quarters of countries will have either an aging population or one that is already senior. As a result, the number of workers aged fifty-five to sixty-four years will increase to represent between 12% and 25% of the total labor force by 2030.

The report also points out that the gender gap in labor market participation is large, especially in emerging countries, but it is diminishing with age across all income levels as policies become more targeted. An aging population impacts societies everywhere, the report tells us, because older people are dependent on the contributions of younger workers to pay into pension schemes. This is another reason why it's good for seniors to remain in the workforce for as long as possible.

Any reluctance that employers and society as a whole have to employ older people must be overcome if everyone is to benefit from the wisdom, experience and knowledge that older people can offer. Research has shown that working into later life is good for the health,[12] so seniors remaining in the workforce has to be a win-win.

Case study: How embracing technology has made senior life easy

In this case study, co-author Carole Railton, who is in her seventies, tells how she has always embraced technology and how doing so has made her life easy.

"At the age of eighteen, I went to work for a well-known IT company as an assistant, then was promoted to supervisor. The department I oversaw consisted of highly qualified computer programmers with degrees. I didn't have a degree, nor did I have the self-confidence to take the job on permanently, even though I had been doing it for six months in a temporary capacity. Instead, I chose to get married and move to Zambia—just so I did not have to take a job. How times have changed! The marriage, unsurprisingly, didn't last long.

"Although I could have seen that move as a failure, I had already learned a lot from my three years working for the IT company. From a relatively young age, I was introduced to modern technology and data processing. I remember telling my father how fast the disk ran on the system we were using. When he didn't believe me, I got permission to take him into the machine room and show him how it all worked. I am talking about the mainframe computers and large systems that were being put into universities and big business at the time.

"During my time with the IT company, I learned about the pay system for the military in the US. I got to program a system that showed all the previous Wimbledon tennis champions through the ages and what the result would be if they all played on the same day. I also got involved with the British Overseas Airways Corporation's (now British Airways) first ticketing system.

"I am old enough to remember the punch cards that were used in computers before disks. Unfortunately, they often fell all over the floor, which meant we had to stack them in order again. My goodness! How inefficient that was when I think back.

"Although my self-esteem was not high at this stage, which wasn't helped by marrying the wrong person, my interest in technology and data processing had been aroused. I had completed a Fortran computer programming course and loved the speed at which things worked.

"As a dyslexic, I had struggled with maths at school, but now I was in my element. Machines did the maths; I just had to collate the information. I had failed the maths test, and the English, too, when I applied for the job with the IT company. Nonetheless, I was employed because I had got 100% in the logic test, thanks to my pragmatic skills.

"My interest in the speed and movement of information (data) continues to this day. I am what is called an 'early adopter,' taking on the latest technology to aid my life and keep up with what is going on in the world. I use Apple devices now. I have an Apple telephone, computer and iPad, but not the watch as I need large print to read. All my products are connected to each other so everything is updated simultaneously, which means that there is no hassle for me and it is easy for me to live an organized life.

"I no longer have to check my spelling when I am writing on my computer as I talk to the machine and it more or less prints out what I am saying. It obviously knows more than I as its spelling is about 98% correct. In fact, I now enjoy the AI-driven facility to talk to all my devices, including my telephone.

"Paying by telephone for public transport is easy. It's just a matter of touching the telephone to a pad at the station gates or as I get on the bus. This makes me feel safe as a senior as I don't need to carry cash or bank cards. Since the touch screen works with facial recognition, there is little chance of anyone else using my smartphone to pay for anything, so I feel my device is secure, which is important at my age.

"I can order food and groceries and book tickets by talking to my telephone. It's like having my own PA. I can also play games on the telephone while waiting for transport, take photos, have a torch at the ready and get directions, among other things.

"If you are not familiar with the apps on a smartphone and don't think you need them, let me assure you that you do. You can call up a map if you get lost and follow the blue dots to get to your destination, all by talking to your telephone. Some of you may be fearful of technology—of computers, smartphones and tablets—but learning how to find your way around it is the same as learning to drive a car. Once you get the hang of it, you will be able to take advantage of the many new things it offers.

"We now have to pay our service providers—such as the telephone, internet or electricity company—online. There are a lot of pluses to paying this way. One of them is that we can talk to automated systems and the system can fill in the forms for us. That really helps me as a dyslexic and will help anyone with declining eyesight, too.

"Thanks to technology, I feel in control of my life. That is why I got involved in writing this book with Lucia, using AI and robots. Technology has done a lot for me, particularly in my recovery from long Covid. It's a luxury to be alive at this time and able to utilize technology, which aids me in every way, every day.

Summary

In this chapter, we have taken a glimpse into what the technological future could look like for seniors. We have covered:

- Why seniors should engage with technology

- Some of the benefits of technology

- What seniors look for in technology

- The importance of training and online courses

- How embracing technology has made life easy for seniors and everyone else

- Why employers need to consider older workers when they're recruiting

Learning about and understanding the latest technology is important for all seniors if they are to find employment, stay in the workforce for as long as possible or even do voluntary work. Employers must realize the potential of the older population and invest in it. They could do this by offering skills training in technology.

Overall, the future for seniors regarding technology, and AI in particular, looks bright, but they must be willing to embrace it. This means they must learn how to use it, and use it well.

8

What's Next
For Technology?

Over the last few years, many companies have been deploying technology, often in the form of AI, in such a way as to help seniors. AI can be used to make the existing operations of organizations and companies more powerful, but it can also be used to develop self-driving cars and VAs, for example, which are designed to make everyone's lives easy to manage.

Some organizations use AI to help sort out content. Google, a subsidiary of multinational technology conglomerate Alphabet, uses AI to filter out spam for users of its email service, Gmail. Amazon uses AI to recommend products to customers, while Netflix uses it to guide content creation and recommendations.

Other organizations use AI to sell specific services. Take IBM, for example. Its AI technology is used in healthcare and financial services, areas in which seniors can benefit.[1] By deploying AI, IBM aims to bring new drugs to market quickly, as well as improving the quality of care. In the financial services market, it uses AI to help clients with regulatory compliance.

This chapter will look at the technology that is being developed and how it could benefit seniors. One area in which seniors will benefit the most is the introduction of near-driverless cars.

Driverless cars

With the aid of technology, seniors will be able to continue to drive long past the age where it would once have been impossible. That said, we have not yet reached the point where cars are completely driverless. What we do have are advanced driver assistance system (ADAS) vehicles with different levels of functionality. In most cases, the driver must remain fully alert, steering when necessary.

Co-author Lucia's late father was able to keep driving up until his death at the age of eighty-seven because his car was equipped with a basic level of automation. A GPS assisted him with directions. A rear-view camera helped him when parking or reversing, and there was cruise control for long-distant driving. If he drifted out of a lane when driving or came too close to another car, a loud beep sounded. He was alerted when he wasn't wearing a seatbelt and the seats were even heated. This type of car is known as partial driving automation. The driver still needs to be in control of the car for steering, accelerating or braking.

Cars that are classified as Levels 3, 4 and 5, as defined by the Society of Automotive Engineers (SAE), are "driverless."[2] This means that the driver does not have to be involved at all in the driving process when the automated features are engaged. BMW intends to bring a Level 3 autonomous car to market in the second half of 2025.[3] At Level 5, the vehicle's ADAS drives all the time. No vehicle manufacturer has designed a car that reaches Level 5 as yet, but this will happen.

One of the biggest challenges to developing self-driving cars is ensuring that they can detect objects on the road correctly. If the car does not make the right assessment, the AI driver could use the brakes or accelerate at the wrong time and cause an accident. When manufacturers have overcome this challenge, driverless vehicles are expected to reduce the number of road traffic accidents significantly, thereby making huge economic saving in terms of the cost of days off work and healthcare. Surveys show that by removing human emotions from the driving process, AI-driven cars could reduce road accidents by 90%.[4]

Self-driving cars have been a boost to companies such as Micron Technology that develop memory chips for use extensively in such cars and smartphones.[5] Other companies are researching AI areas like near-memory and in-memory computing, embedded non-volatile memory technologies, 3D integration and error-resilient computing which impacts the memory of self-driving cars.[6]

Near-memory and in-memory computing fall under the heading of "memory-centric" computing. The aim of these is to bring the "memory closer or integrate it into processing tasks" to boost the memory of computer systems. They can be used for different applications, social media being one.[7]

Other ways of deploying AI

We are all encouraged to use social media and seniors that use social media, whether it be to avoid isolation or for whatever reason, will need to become accustomed to the fact that many platforms apply AI technology to newsfeeds and advertising algorithms. This means that all users, including seniors, receive an increasing number of targeted advertisements.

AI technology is building and developing the metaverse, a digital world in which users live, socialize, play and interact. The metaverse is used extensively by fashion designers such as Balenciaga, Adidas, Nike and Gucci.[8] Instead of shoppers entering a bricks-and-mortar store, they can access digital avatars that are dressed up by consumers in the metaverse and make purchases, often using non-fungible tokens (NFTs). In 2022 alone, NFT sales on the metaverse amounted to US$137.5 million.[9] An NFT is a unique digital identifier and uses blockchain technology to record when and how they are used. An NFT is like currency in that it can be used by another person, but only if it is transferred by the owner. In this way, they can be sold or traded.[10] Even if seniors do not use NFTs themselves, the younger generation are now using them in the metaverse so it is helpful for seniors to become accustomed to the jargon.

The use of electronic signatures will also become increasingly common. AI technology is deployed to ensure this is safe and secure. These signatures are frequently used by real estate agents and solicitors, so seniors are likely to use them in their engagements. The e-signature market is estimated to be worth US$25.2 billion by 2027, according to analysts.[11]

Seniors are likely to benefit from AI when they call a customer services number if they need help from their bank or telephone company, for example. Often, the caller is forced to wait on the telephone, sometimes for a couple of hours, before an agent picks up the line, so the use of AI is expected to speed up the experience.[12] AI allows the company to use software that recognizes a customer's voice and gives them a tailored experience.

AI will help seniors who are reliant on care, particularly in the post-pandemic labor shortage. Carers can concentrate on caring for seniors while workflow automation deals with administrative tasks, such as maintaining staff records, conducting resident family surveys, verification of new hires and keeping up with the financials.

Predictions about AI

Many people are making predictions about how AI could help humanity in the future. Most of these predictions cover retail and health, and some are expected to impact seniors more or less immediately. Other developments will require a wait-and-see approach.

Immediate developments are likely to include:

- Increased automation in the way we live and work. Our everyday needs will be affected—that is food, water, air and love. Take love for example. Part of finding love with a partner is learning about their behaviors, their values and how much energy they have and use in a relationship. Already we have dating sites where we can investigate potential partners, and as AI gathers data there will be more information on each individual so the dating process will be shortened. More detail gives us the chance to advance more rapidly with relationships as we already have the basics.

- Pathways made of illuminated material so that walking at night will be easy and safe, especially for seniors.

- People globally will be fitted with a microchip the size of a grain of rice, often inserted into the thumb. In Sweden, thousands already have microchips inserted into their hands to make their lives more convenient, easily accessing their homes, offices and gyms by swiping their hands against digital readers.[13] Chips can also be used to store emergency contact details, social-media profiles, e-tickets for events and rail journeys, and vaccine passports if we see another era where vaccine mandates are put in place.

Overall, information that is readily available will help everyone in their day-to-day lives, seniors in particular. It gives us the chance to advance our lives more successfully and quickly. We can find out what the temperature is in a location we are about to visit, what time the bus is coming that we are going to get into town, how to treat a medical condition as it arrives to stop it progressing. Having all this information in advance completely changes our lives. It speeds up what we need to know and helps us on to the next stage of a project.

Let's look at some of the sectors AI is expected to change in the not-so-distant future.

Retail

Huge developments are expected in the retail sector, which means seniors will have to adapt. These developments vary from fashion shows, with the industry making moves to eliminate waste through digital fashion, to the individual online shopping experience.

Many of these changes will affect not just where customers shop, but how they do it. Although these developments are predicted to make our lives easier in the long term than they are now, seniors may have to adjust to not going to the supermarket. Co-author Lucia's father would go to the supermarket most days for something to do, but there are many other ways to pass your time and socialize. (We have covered some things you can do in this book, such as re-entering the employment market and embracing social media. For example, doing a course to improve your IT knowledge is a great way to occupy your time productively and equip yourself with the skills to thrive in the modern world.)

One of the main catalysts for change in the retail sector was the Covid-19 pandemic. Shops needed to be innovative to reduce physical interactions, so the popularity of online shopping soared, contactless payments were the norm, and digital technologies like AI, quick response (QR) codes, track and trace technology, VR and AR became commonplace.

By using AI, ML and deep learning, all retailers can provide their customers with an efficient personal service. It is likely that the use of AI will increase in the retail sector as a whole and retailers will become more centralized, particularly in terms of ordering products and tracking customer developments, but to date, some retailers have been reluctant to invest in AI technology because of the costs involved. This is likely to change because, as stores generate more data, they will get better insights about customers' behavior and how their needs can be best met. Seniors will most certainly benefit from these changes.

Take Amazon, for example. Amazon has a wide choice of products and its delivery and returns policies are easy to use and efficient. With the help of AI, goods are often shipped overnight. Consequently, customers now expect deliveries to arrive in hours or days rather than weeks. In its overall business, Amazon has been highly reliant on AI for growth.

Supermarkets will benefit from the use of AI, leading to less human contact and potentially guarding against another pandemic. Robots could carry out food deliveries and may even make the food as well. If this happens, it is likely to mean more home-cooked meals that are delivered and lower production costs than we have now, which would benefit seniors, many of whom are living on a budget due to low pension payments.

With new technology, seniors are already able to shop from the comfort of their homes. Japanese cosmetics company Shiseido uses hands-free technology to analyze skin and offer personalized services remotely.[14] Burberry, a UK fashion house, has opened its first social retail store in Shenzhen, China, where shoppers can interact with the store on social media, using messaging and calling app WeChat, or in person.[15] A mini-program is unlocked via WeChat and customers can book one of three fitting rooms, pre-select clothes and try them on virtually. They can even select their preferred choice of music.

In restaurants, the use of robots is likely to become increasingly common. Waiters could even be robots and the reduction in overheads could be passed on to customers, meaning more people will be able to eat out more often.

Education

Covid-19 changed the virtual learning space and this is likely to continue as educational institutions open up online. As remote teaching becomes the norm in schools and universities around the world, seniors will be able to learn more courses from the comfort of their own home.

The role of teachers will inevitably change. They will still be needed in an online environment for such things as planning lessons and supervising the classroom, but some teachers are complaining that this has made their work more difficult, not less.

In the future, online learning will mean that teachers at all levels will make greater use of digital applications and students' needs could be personalized.

Healthcare

Healthcare is another area in which the use of AI is developing rapidly. AI in healthcare brings together research and medicine. Although we discussed healthcare in Chapter Four, here we will concentrate on what the developments in the sector may mean in the future.

Take Hong Kong-based Deep Longevity, for example. This company develops AI not only to track the rate of aging at the molecular, cellular, tissue, organ, system, physiological and psychological levels, but also for the emerging field of longevity medicine. Deep Longevity, through a research partnership with

Human Longevity, provides various aging clocks to physicians and researchers.[16] The ability to predict age using these clocks will become more common which will perhaps allow the medical profession to diagnose issues and find ways to ensure that a person lives longer.

Sleep is another area where there are significant AI developments. Although you may think that products to allow seniors to improve their sleep would make sense, since so many people have told us that as they age, they tend to sleep less and falling asleep becomes more difficult, there are surprisingly few products on the market to combat bad sleep for seniors. Part of the reason is that monitoring sleep can be difficult.

Bed manufacturer Bryte has introduced what it calls the "restorative" bed, featuring a mattress that can make seniors sleep soundly.[17] It is based on the belief that if sleep is fragmented, it is not restorative, so the mattress aims to combat broken sleep patterns. Its website says: "Informed by science and powered by artificial intelligence, it [the mattress] pinpoints each person's unique needs at any moment." These needs are things like regulating body temperature and easing pain points. Several hotels are already using these mattresses.

Eight Sleep, an American technology company, has also introduced a mattress that's powered by AI.[18] It aims not only to give you good-quality sleep, but to make you feel more refreshed when you wake up. Eight Sleep syncs its smart mattresses with an AI-powered sleep coach app that delivers insights and makes recommendations based on a person's sleep history. These recommendations include adjusting environmental conditions, such as how much light is in the room or its temperature.

Several products designed to enable people to get a good night's sleep are in various stages of development. In July 2021, researchers at the University of Sheffield developed AI technology that can monitor snoring levels and identify sleep disorders.[19] AI is now being commercialized through a new iOS app SoundSleep that enables people to track their breathing while they sleep using their smartphone and helps them discover the causes, factors and solutions to snoring and disorders such as sleep apnea.[20]

The Apple Watch can automatically track sleep quality if the user wears it to bed. The information collected is then used to make personalized recommendations for how to get better rest. Apps like Sonic Sleep use a phone's microphone to assess background noise, and then an AI-powered algorithm is employed to pick out the right audio to mask it. Sleep.ai says it can detect sleep apnea, snoring and teeth grinding by analyzing sound samples.[21]

Tochtech, a Canadian company, has developed Sleepsense, a non-wearable tracker that allows caregivers to monitor the sleep patterns of seniors overnight.[22] Sleepsense is designed to alert caregivers when a senior experiences a health risk, such as an abnormal heart or breathing rate, during sleep. About the size of a cell phone, the Sleepsense device is placed under the leg or frame of the bed. It uses high-precision sensors and algorithm technology to measure ballistocardiogram waves and record heart and respiration rates. Notifications and alarms of any changes go to mobile devices carried by a caregiver or a staff member in a care home.

Online medical consultations will become common, accelerating a trend that started during the Covid-19 pandemic, with patients using software like Zoom or Skype to speak with doctors remotely rather than visiting a surgery physically. This method has some benefits, for example, seniors won't have to travel, but people have complained that if they consult doctors this way, they won't be able to have a physical examination. As fewer people work within health services around the world, it is likely that robots will increasingly do medical interventions.

Co-author Carole recently needed to deal with a doctor in the UK. Here, she tells us of her experience.

"I had a frozen shoulder, so I called my local surgery and spoke to the receptionist. A doctor called me back and asked me a set of questions, and then recommended some exercises. It would have been quicker, easier, less time-consuming and less costly for the UK's NHS if I had been able to tap into a program that asked specific questions such as, 'Have you lost strength in your left/right arm? Have you any pain in your legs? Is one side of your face drooping?' The program could have contained numerous exercises for different conditions."

Tracking and longevity

A watch-like device called CarePredict from a US-based company can indicate serious issues in seniors before they happen.[23] This also helps families and caregivers know what an older person is up to— whether they are visiting a friend or playing a game such as bowls or at a doctor's appointment—without them actually being there with the senior. On its website, CarePredict says that its technology will allow people to detect often imperceptible early signs of aging, which is important in making the correct diagnoses, alert carers when a senior needs help and recommend relevant interventions.

One of the areas tracking technology is used, and is helpful, is in preventing falls. The National Council on Aging (NCA) says that one in four Americans aged sixty-five and older falls each year and that every nineteen minutes an older person dies from a fall. Statistics show that this figure is similar in other developed countries.[24] These falls are preventable, with the right glasses, the right exercises and the right tracking devices, the NCA says.

AI has the potential to ensure that everybody lives long and healthy lives via "longevity medicine." CarePredict says that aging, tracking and picking up-to-the-minute changes that occur in the human body, such as temperature or pulse rate, and spotting patterns that medicines or further AI could be designed to counter.

PAs and health bots are likely to become more commonly used by seniors. These companions have the capacity to recommend therapy, remind patients about any medication they need to take, and identify and respond to patients who fall, all of which will ease the pressure on caregivers. Since humans have a strong need for relationships, they have the capacity to form bonds with things, such as art, places and, of course, robots, in the absence of living beings.

Some technology is designed to keep seniors safe. Alarm systems to deter intruders and stoves that alert people if they're too hot have been around for a long time, but incorporating AI that helps people make decisions to live longer and better lives is new. For example, AI can help select suitable recipes, measure body temperature, and let people know if they need to take their medication.

Advertising

Arguably, brands in Hong Kong and Singapore are the forerunners of using advertising concepts that build offline and online audiences, but advertising and marketing will become more bespoke and personal the world over. In Singapore, Near, a user- and location-data company, is "partnering with newly rebranded SMRT transit company media arm Stellar Ace to enable retargeting of audiences around a brand's OOH [out-of-home] advertisements through mobile, to drive footfall to nearby retail stores."[25]

By adopting this technology, Near can target customers with specific messaging at a specific time, such as a meal deal at lunchtime. Those who click on the advertisement are directed to the nearest restaurant offering the deal. This technology allows advertisers to obtain data-driven media-planning tools and customers to receive data-triggered digital content.

It is likely that there will be an increasing number of video advertising products. These are contextual video adverts available on cell phones that will be updated daily. The user is likely to get more targeted information than they would otherwise receive about a product, or its competitors' products, such as changes in price or special promotions, for example.

Another likelihood is that our thoughts will increasingly be tracked—which, to a certain extent, they seem to be already. For example, when we are talking about buying a product while surfing on social media, adverts for that product magically appear, or Siri or Alexa interrupts a conversation without prompting, offering a deal for that product.

All of these benefits can enhance and support our everyday living, from keeping us safe and well to making our decisions easier as we have more relevant information available.

Summary

This chapter has looked at the technology that is being developed and how it could benefit seniors. We have discussed:

- Autonomous cars
- Healthcare
- Longevity of life
- Education
- Companionship

- Advertising

- Retail

As you can see, these are all areas that affect the everyday lives of most people. The world is only going to get more technical, so make sure you're not left behind.

9

How Technology Affects Body Language

Body language is all about interaction with other humans, whether it be in person or on screen. Body language gives insights about a person much more than the voice does. It never lies; it is the spoken word that lies. The future of body language will lead people to interact more with other technologies, including robots.

Online communication and the tools that make it possible are having a profound impact on society. Great success is being achieved with robots understanding who you are and where you are in life at a specific moment, just by reading your body language. They even try to coax you to be in a relaxed state before they do things for you, because being relaxed and stress free helps humans to do everything better.

This chapter will consider how our body language has changed and must continue to change as societies become more reliant on technological devices. It will look at the shift from personal to automated behaviors, what changes technology might bring in the future and the ways in which body language will evolve as a consequence.

Some robots show empathy

How we move about, look and listen is changing as so much is being done for us. We are already using equipment that listens for us or to us. Spotify chooses music for us, shops organize what to show us that fits in with our lifestyle and we can control our heating so it's warm when we arrive home—wonderful when it's freezing outside.

Many people say that robots can't be like humans because they have no feelings. Times have changed. Robots are now equipped with AI, but the first robots were not equipped with it. Robots are also equipped with empathetic technology, which allows them to keep an eye on what people do. They react to changes in movement and, believe it or not, they feel, too. Previously, robots could not understand the feelings and changes that might occur in a human because of environmental issues—whether they're at home or in a restaurant, for example. They are now being programmed to feel—there is more work to be done so that they can imitate humans, however. Empathy is paramount in the development of robots and their understanding of humans; robots will help humans to improve their lives as they and humans become more like each other.

The fact that robots are already reacting to movement is important because the way humans feel is conveyed not only verbally, but also through gestures and movements. This means that robots can act more like and integrate better with humans. Soon they will be able to smell. But no matter how sophisticated robots become, humans are always a step ahead.

Empathetic technology understands our internal condition and decides what to do next to enhance our situation. I guess you could say it uses ML to further human development.

Interacting on a screen and with robots

As a consequence of the Covid-19 pandemic, more communication happens on screen than ever before. It is important for seniors to utilize new on-screen body-language skills so they can communicate with each other and with robots. It takes less than a day to reprogram a robot with new skills and the more advanced ones will already be reprogramming themselves, so it makes sense for seniors to be ready and prepared to adapt their communication skills so they can maintain their position in the world. Our body language must change so we can connect and influence others, and there's no reason why seniors can't be at the forefront of this change.

Visual communication has always been our first point of influence as a species. Our interaction with other people is one of our most important daily behaviors, whether it is face-to-face or digital. Dress, location, even the artwork in our home defines our culture and our experience of life.

One of the consequences of the increased use of video technology is that humans are more restricted in their body movements. We require a different body-language skill when speaking on a screen than that of an in-person interaction. On screen, we have to sit still and concentrate, which can manifest itself as staring.

Peripheral vision is also restricted on a screen. We can only see the person we are talking to and not their surroundings, such as what their desk looks like; we're expected to look directly at the other person for the entire time that we are communicating on screen. That said, the use of video technology has helped to reduce frustration. The reason some people experienced telephone rage was because they couldn't see the person they were talking to— Alexander Graham Bell has a lot to answer for. Video calling has changed that to a certain extent, but nonetheless, we can still get frustrated.

Modern on-screen body-language skills require humans to achieve a presence while creating an instant positive impact on the person or people they're speaking to. To do this, look into the eye of the person you're talking to on the left-hand side of the body—but do check that your image is not reversed before you practice this. This will really help you connect with that person on a deep level because the left-hand side of the body is the receiving side and the right-hand side the giving one. This is why Europeans stretch out their right arm to shake hands, demonstrating open behavior and giving to the other person.

Posture and breathing

The use of the screen has had a big impact on posture, especially for seniors. This is exacerbated by the fact that our experience of communication for most of our lives has been largely face-to-face, which means adapting to a screen-only experience can take longer than it does for a younger person. Sitting at a screen can also stop us as seniors getting as much exercise as we should, and exercise is something that we all need to stay healthy and youthful.

The importance of good posture cannot be overestimated, particularly for seniors as we usually move more slowly than younger people and may take short cuts with our posture. We lose flexibility and become stiffer as we age and may even drop a few centimeters in height as the discs in the back flatten. These changes mean we walk more slowly, use cars or public transport more often, and look for accommodation without stairs. Although using our bodies less may seem the easy and time-saving option as we grow older, if we want to enhance longevity, it's important to move.

Posture is the key to life, breathing and happiness. You can tell if someone is sad or unhappy because they tilt their head down; they literally look down because they are down. If you have a permanently stooping posture, you are likely to be unhappy about life as a result. This is often the reason older people are seen as grumpy.

Co-author Carole remembers her mother telling her to pull her shoulders back and carry her satchel correctly when she was going to school. Her mother said nothing is more important than posture as it can reveal what you are feeling, your health history and whether you are stressed or relaxed, but now it's not Carole's teachers who are reading these signals; it's technology.

In the future, robots equipped with AI will be able to guide the everyday movements of seniors, reminding them when their posture is not as good as it should be—if they lean too far forward, for example. Products like the award-winning posture brace worn by the UK's *Strictly Come Dancing* contestants, to straighten posture while allowing the user to breathe easily, will become more commonplace.[1] Since the shoulders are pulled back, the wearer has more flexibility. There are products in development that tease our muscles with electrodes, and then regenerate them.

Breathing is an important component of body language. We can only live for three minutes without breathing, apart from pearl divers who can last for five minutes. We can tell so much from breathing. The way someone breathes tells us if they are stressed, happy or sexually fulfilled. We only need to sit next to someone on an airplane and hear them sigh, and we know instantly that they are fed up.

Most people think that mimicking the body language of others is the way to influence them, but in fact, it is how we breathe toward them. Mimicking the body language of the person in front of us doesn't work if that person is depressed or stressed, for example. We too would spiral into despair and have no chance of influencing them, unless we have been schooled in how to do this. Breathing as a communication tool is amazing. When we get excited, we breathe quickly; when we are tired, we breathe slowly. Understanding and copying someone's breathing patterns is the best way to influence that person. There is no surer way to get what we want from someone than to do this. The impact is amazing: robots will learn to emulate our breathing patterns.

When Carole is teaching, she shows students how mimicking breathing is an intimate and successful way of getting on an even keel with someone. It's not easy to do, but with practice, anyone can utilize this technique; some hypnotists use it when hypnotizing their clients. For this reason, if they are to communicate with and influence humans, robots must be able to breathe. Without breathing, they will fail in detailed body-language analysis.

The importance of eyes

Scientists at the Hong Kong University of Science and Technology have developed the world's first artificial 3D eye.[2] This eye has capabilities better than existing bionic eyes and, in some cases, exceeds those of the human eye, thus bringing vision to humanoid robots. The eye also brings new hope to patients with a visual impairment.

A simple fact that we must all acknowledge is that we are using our eyes differently when we are communicating on screen. Increasingly, we are seeing other people's eyes before any other part of their body. It's interesting, therefore, to think about how eyes will work in robots.

Robots will be able to detect if someone has dementia or another life-debilitating disease from observing the pupils in their eyes, possibly learning more about a person's health condition than doctors as a result. They will be able to assess body language and read how humans respond to different situations, soon adding the reading of eyes to their knowledge bank.

Eyes are key in body language. In the Victorian era, women used to put belladonna in their eyes to enlarge their pupils. Large pupils are a sign you like something, so they did it to attract men. Now poker players wear dark glasses to cover their eyes during tournaments so that their opponents cannot read whether they have a good or bad hand.

One thing co-author Carole is known for is her training on how to look someone in the eye. Previously, people were taught to look into both eyes, using a triangle that included the nose when talking to others. This is a threatening pose. If you really want action, it's best to look someone in their left eye, the receiving side of the body.

Robots are aware of this, so when a robot is talking to you and looking into your left eye, be aware that you are being checked out. The merging of humans and robots will run smoothly when robots do this as they will achieve a deep condition with us. We humans are then likely to respond as we would when talking to another human.

Other factors in body language

Although robots are able to determine what we are saying and doing, one area that needs work is assessing body temperature. Nowadays, there are thermostats in our homes that we can control from anywhere. The thermostat can be set to come on when the surrounding temperature gets to a certain level, but how does the machine know if we are feeling cold or hot?

Co-author Carole's friend always feels warm while Carole herself generally feels cold, even when they're in the same environment.

Although a robot can learn from a human's past experience of being hot and cold, it does not know how that affects each one of us physically or mentally at a particular moment. To make the right assessment, a robot needs to know if the intention of a human or humans is to sleep, rest or wake up. This requires empathetic technology so robots assess our needs by looking at our internal state and responding accordingly.

Through social media, it is now possible to enter the metaverse. Meta (previously Facebook) has a system where you start off in a blank room and can tell it what you want to experience. This way, you can be transported anywhere at will. For example, you may want to be on a beach in a hot location with palm trees and calypso music, sitting in a deckchair exchanging conversation with the locals. Meta will create this for you instantly, along with immediate translation of the local languages.

In 2009, Nudge, an impartial financial education company, started data-driven learning through body language.[3] It uses behavioral psychology and data to inform end users of financial action to take to gain access to benefits, all personalized as a nudge reminder. Nudges can be received via SMS, email or WhatsApp.

At this stage, not everything works perfectly with online video-calling services such as Skype, Zoom and the like but it is a hugely useful tool. It isn't possible to read the subtle body-language signals of others nor see their full location, but when communications are face-to-face, humans take in not only the person and what they are wearing, but the ambience of the situation, attire and their environment. We are able to look around a room and see pictures, books or furniture—all of which gives us clues to the person we are talking to. When we are using online conference tools, we do not have this advantage.

Online video-calling tools require us to look at a small space—the screen—for a concentrated time. This focus and concentration are what causes us to feel tired after a call online. We normally divert our eyes when we are communicating in real life and we notice what is going on around us. In a screen-to-screen communication we rely directly on the small image in front of us to receive information.

Despite the negatives to video communication, it has been a major development and the advantages of communicating with one another in such a way will become greater over time.

How face recognition will develop

In the past, robots have found it difficult to judge humans by visuals, preferring to work on what is being said, but a new era has dawned. Robots are now comfortable with facial recognition and body language. They must be. After all, the first thing we see when meeting people is their body language and facial expressions. Subtle observations give us clues to what is going on in the minds of other people.

The global facial recognition market size was valued at US$3.86 billion in 2020 and is expected to expand at a compound annual growth rate of 15.4% from 2021 to 2028, according to Grand View Research.[4] Just think of how you can open your computer by showing it your face or use your thumbprint to unlock different programs—a great way of reducing the need for the much-dreaded passwords. Safety in international travel is improved thanks to digital photos being matched to the real you; banks identify you against a claimed identity; and you can get into futuristic buildings with facial recognition. Social-media sites recognize you and fill in your photo accordingly. You can open a new bank account by sitting at home and having your passport and telephone to hand. The system copies your passport and takes a picture of you to prove you are the passport owner. When co-author Carole did this recently with a fully digital bank, the whole process took eight minutes, including reading the terms and conditions.

Filling in forms online can often be done automatically as the computer has stored all the details and facial recognition can do the rest. Facial recognition is also being used in telemedicine. (For more on how technology is benefiting healthcare and financial services, see Chapters Four and Five.)

Liar, liar!

Soon, robots will be able to read if someone is telling lies or not. No human body-language guru will ever be able to recognize every lie, but with the advancements in technology, robots are being programmed with knowledge from around the globe about how humans react and use their body language. As a result, robots will spot when someone is lying, whatever their heritage. It will become virtually impossible to lie to them without them knowing.

Organizations such as the FBI in the United States have knowledge programmed into robots, thereby making them the best instant body-language readers in the world. The ability of these programmed robots to read body language will mean they can give us information in the best way possible to suit our personality type.

Co-author Carole's parents always taught her to be honest and she is grateful for her ability to tell the truth, which is especially important in her occupation as a body-language consultant. She has worked for multinationals and small, progressive companies, interacted with many societies, security industries and management consultants, and has always been able to read people's body language and they hers. Now, though, robots are already being programmed with body-language skills that Carole has taken forty years to acquire and technology can be programmed with body-language skills to help seniors.

What else to consider

Size, because it indicates power, is an important factor in body language. Indeed, size can determine how robots interact with us. Historically, height has influenced how well people have done in society, as has the size of their home. People who have not done so well live in small accommodation while the richer, more successful members of society have large houses or penthouse apartments. Robots understand this and will treat people accordingly so must also take into account that some seniors may choose to down-size after their children have flown the nest.

Hand movements are important; so much of how we express ourselves is with our hands. We use them to enhance what we are saying and to direct others. Our first interaction with a stranger is generally shaking hands or hugging, but this is changing. While Carole was working in Germany fifteen years ago, people in other countries were connected to a machine via their skin. It was possible to see from the feedback what emotional state they were in. Some were stressed, others relaxed, and Carole and her colleagues determined how this information could be used. This information is now being used to develop AI systems.

Seniors need company as loneliness quickly leads to declining health. That's why many apps and messengers allow a person to create an avatar. Avatars create a human connection in a virtual world.[5] Despite the expected explosion in the growth of AI and its use in body language and facial recognition, many seniors are still not adopting its benefits. Often, they feel considerable reluctance to migrate from old to new systems; transformation is never easy, but if we totally understand it, we stand a much better chance of implementing and using new technology successfully than if we don't.

There is no doubt that all societies are in the middle of behavioral changes, but none is more prevalent than developments in body language and facial recognition. Let's wake up and use the AI that has been built to support us. If we understand how digital body language will benefit us, we will move forward and not fear the future. This understanding brings us to an acknowledgment and acceptance of AI.

The future of body language

In the future, it is likely that environments will be simulated—perhaps using VR for a more immersive experience—so people will have to become better at reading others and acting instinctively. Currently, to utilize VR, we have to wear goggles and/or glasses, often embedded with tiny computer screens.

Soon, it will be possible to create the environment that we want via our computer. Having choices about our surroundings can bring us closer to other people, making communication and life in general easier than they are now. It will be the norm for us to communicate in human-made environments that will enhance our feelings of goodwill. As we saw earlier in the chapter, Meta (formerly Facebook) already allows us to create our preferred environment on screen.

Computer chip maker Nvidia Corp is building its Omniverse platform for connecting 3D worlds into a shared virtual universe.[6] It says Omniverse, which is used for projects like creating simulations of real-world buildings and factories, is the "plumbing" on which metaverses could be built.

Flat screens will vanish. When it comes to advertisements, our experiences will be similar to those in countries like Singapore and

Hong Kong, where large 3D projections move outwards toward us so we believe they can touch us, even though they are just images directed to our space at that moment in time. Cinemas have been producing films that send out images to the audience for a while now. When Carole was last in the USA, she attended an event where the images that came close to her in 3D included smells and water to enhance the experience.

These changes will impact body language and how people interact with one another. When we have designed our own environments, we will be able to communicate more effectively and quickly in a universe we prefer. All the data from that communication will be programmed into robots, speeding it up even further. We will, therefore, need to hone our behavioral skills, including how we interact with robots, to ensure we are communicating at the same level. Robots will accumulate data from previous interactions.

Summary

In this chapter, we have looked at the fascinating subject of body language, co-author Carole Railton's area of expertise, concentrating on how the way we communicate both consciously and subconsciously will evolve with the development of new technology. We have covered:

- How robots are learning to show empathy via empathetic technology

- How robots use ML to further human development

- Using and adapting body-language skills to communicate well on screen

- The importance of good posture

- The role breathing plays in communication

- How and why we use our eyes when communicating on screen

- The way in which robots will learn to recognize how temperature will affect different people in different ways and at different times

- How face recognition will develop

- The role of AI-powered robots in detecting lies from a person's body language

- What the future holds for body language

Already, robots are starting to react to human feelings and act like humans. As this technology advances, it can only be good news for humans, particularly seniors, because robots will recognize our needs and take the stresses of life away from us, leaving us free to enjoy our lives.

Conclusion

The demographics of the world are changing, and quickly. Soon, people who are over sixty-five will outnumber those who are younger, according to the United Nations.[1]

Indeed, the *Mail Online* says there are 11.1 million people over sixty-five in the United Kingdom—that's one in six people and means there are more over sixty-fives than children for first time in history, according to the latest census figures.[2] Moreover, despite the Covid pandemic hitting older people hard, there are now more than half a million over-nineties in the UK. That's up a quarter in a decade, the article states. This older population is indicative of what is happening all over the world and is confirmed by the World Population Prospects 2019.[3] By 2050, one in six people in the world will be over the age of sixty-five, up from one in eleven in 2019.[4]

For this reason, policy makers must make decisions in the best interests of the older demographic. Seniors want to be embraced by society, whether they are doing everyday things, are members of the workforce or are entrepreneurs. Discrimination is an issue that needs to be tackled now.

Ageism often comes about as a result of the belief that seniors cannot handle technology. If we as seniors fail to embrace technology, it means that society will not benefit from the experience, skills and wisdom that we have accumulated over the years. For employers, younger people may be up to date with the latest technology, but seniors are often more knowledgeable and, with the right training, can be brought up to speed quickly and easily with technology. Training is a must for employees of any age, but it will be good for the brand and the overall image of a business to employ seniors.

Those who are alive now are at the forefront of technological change. Developments in AI and robots have been amazing, with more to come. The Covid pandemic hastened changes and the take up of new technologies, such as video conferencing. In the next few years, there is likely to be even greater and more rapid change, with the developments in the field of technology and AI that we've discussed in this book coming to fruition.

Some of the technological changes to which seniors are currently having to adapt, such as smartphones, are likely to become obsolete. According to the CEO of Nokia, Pekka Lundmark, speaking at Davos in May 2022, smartphones are likely to be overtaken by smart glasses and other devices that will be worn on the face. He predicts that this will happen by 2030.[5] Some of these devices will be built into the body.

Seniors not only need to adapt to new technology, but they also need to embrace it enthusiastically. Technology can bring so many advantages to seniors, allowing them to lead comfortable and independent lives. Manufacturers are already designing digital devices with seniors in mind. Seniors can benefit from everything from near-driverless cars to retail outlets that don't require payment on checkout, to the way food is frozen and cooked, to cameras that allow the house to be checked when they're on holiday.

There are hundreds, if not thousands, of factors and innovations that are going to change the world for seniors. In this book, we have looked at what is going on now and what we might expect in the immediate future. It's time to utilize and be amazed by what is coming. There are likely to be changes that we have not even considered; things we cannot imagine now. It is a good time to be alive; to be part of the behavioral shift that is happening in society; to be involved in the technological changes taking place. The Fourth Industrial Revolution has already started and the way people communicate is changing. Technological developments, including AI, will be part of that change.

Lucia and Carole, the authors, sincerely hope that their book will help you achieve the first step on the ladder of knowledge that will carry you forward successfully so you can live out your life in the best way possible. Appreciate yourself for getting this far. Soon, you will be able to support others in their endeavors to develop themselves and get the most out of life.

Help And Support

There are several places around the world where seniors can be introduced to the latest technology, including computer software, or trained to use it effectively. It is important to keep up with technology and to be digitally savvy if you want to engage with society in your senior years.

We have listed the resources on offer in different countries.

United States of America

The USA has many places that offer courses or one-to-one tuition to seniors so that they become more au fait with technology. Some of them are technology companies themselves; others are community groups.

Koenig Solutions claims to be the world's largest provider of certificated online courses, technology courses among them. The company operates in several countries as well as the United States.

If you don't fancy joining a course, you can have one-to-one tutoring instead. For details of all the courses on offer, go to www. koenig-solutions.com. Contact details are: info@koenig-solutions. com.

SeniorNet is a non-profit organization focused on education. It trains people so that the gap between seniors and technology becomes narrower. To learn more about its programs, it is necessary to sign up for its affiliate program at programs@seniornet.org.

The LeadingAge Center for Aging Services Technologies (CAST) aims to expedite the development, evaluation and adoption of emerging technologies that can improve the aging experience. For more information, contact info@leadingage.org or go to the website at www.leadingage.org.

Older Adult Network Online Learning Center, part of Greenwich House in New York (www.greenwichhouse.org/older-adult-centers/senior-centers/online-learning-center/#classes), offers a host of online programs and other resources for older people. You can master the tech basics by following the link on the website to Senior Planet. Call the hotline on 920-666-1959.

Massachusetts AI and Technology Center (https://massaitc. org/technology-identification-training-core) is a center for aging and Alzheimer's disease. It is a collaboration with the National Institute of Aging that encourages the use of AI technologies in the home to support healthy aging, principally for those with Alzheimer's disease. Its technology and identification training core pursues projects that not only answer scientific questions, but ensure each person makes the most of the latest technologies available.

Bridging Apps (https://bridgingapps.org/seniors/social-networker) lists some technologies that seniors might find useful, from reading, game and memory apps to mental-health and vision apps. It is headquartered in Houston, Texas. Get in touch on 713-838-9050 x 383.

Older Adults Technology Services (OATS) (https://oats.org) collaborates with **AARP** (www.aarp.org/aarp-foundation/our-work/income/info-2022/aarp-foundation-to-provide-free-digital-skills-training.html) to provide technological and digital skills training to seniors. Until January 2024, programs and services to help in a time of financial hardship will be rolled out into eight states: Arizona, Georgia, Illinois, Louisiana, North Carolina, Pennsylvania, South Carolina and Texas.

AARP (www.aarp.org) is a US-based non-profit nonpartisan organization with a membership of nearly 38 million. It helps people turn their goals and dreams into real possibilities, strengthens communities and fights for the issues that matter most to families such as healthcare, employment and income security, retirement planning, affordable utilities and protection from financial abuse. The AARP Foundation is an affiliated charity that provides security, protection and empowerment to older people in need with support from thousands of volunteers, donors and sponsors. AARP has staffed offices in all fifty US states, the District of Columbia, Puerto Rico and the US Virgin Islands.

Codecademy (www.codecademy.com) is focused on training people to code computers. Training is free and online. It is not focused on a particular age group.

MIT-Harvard Business School. Programs can be designed to meet the needs of a particular group or individual. MIT encourages partnerships. To find out more about its technology and innovation acceleration program, go to https://mit-xpro-online-education. emeritus.org/technology-innovation-acceleration.

UC Berkeley School of Information (www.ischool.berkeley. edu). Courses for all age groups are available here to enable a person to pursue an advanced degree in IT.

MIT Sloan School of Management (https://cambridge-online-executive-education.emeritus.org/chief-technology-officer-programme). Like UC Berkeley, the courses here are geared toward obtaining a degree in IT.

Healthy Aging (www.paho.org/en/healthy-aging). This is a Pan-American health organization (PAHO) that aims to ensure that everyone ages healthily.

The Milken Institute Center for Aging (https://
milkeninstitute.org). This US-based organization is part of the
Milken Institute. It is a nonprofit nonpartisan think tank that helps
people build meaningful lives.

Canada

Tech Coaches (https://techcoaches.ca/contact-us). This
company teaches older people about technology and offers "live,
online learning sessions for end users and educators, as well
as ongoing support." The solutions allow members to keep up
with the latest technology. Members can learn everything about
technology from the basics, learning about Zoom and other video
technologies, as well as how to avoid scammers. Learners can also
become "tech champions," teaching others what they have learned.

Seniors Tech Services (www.seniorstechservices.ca) offers
computer training for adults. You can go learn all the skills you
need to help you in everyday living.

Calgary services (www.calgary.ca/social-services/seniors/
using-technology.html) is the city of Calgary's website providing
a list of organizations that offer technological training services
to seniors, including Cyber-Seniors, Deaf and Hear Alberta,
Step Ahead Program, GLUU Technology Society, Connected
Canadians, and a link to AARP about accessibility tools on
smartphones.

Connected Canadians (www.connectedcanadians.ca/
contact) is a non-profit organization connecting older adults with
technology training and support. This is by way of one-to-one
training, workshops and online.

Tech Smart Senior by STEM Camp (https://techsmartsenior. stemcamp.ca) offers a range of courses for seniors online. "General knowledge" includes courses on how to search the internet, how to use abbreviations and internet language and how to avoid scams; "Shopping" includes how to use PayPal, and how to shop using Amazon, Walmart, and Uber Eats; and there are several other categories such as "Transportation" (Uber and Lyft), "Entertainment" (Netflix, YouTube, Audiobooks), "Gaming" and "Communication" (how to use FaceTime, set up a Gmail account, use Zoom and create a Facebook account).

Center for Learning & Living (www.clandl.org) provides a range of courses for seniors. Among the courses being taught are those on technology such as "Online Purchase Scams & Financial Fraud: Red Flags and Pitfalls to Avoid."

The Digital Literacy Exchange Program, Canada (https:// ised-isde.canada.ca/site/digital-literacy-exchange-program/en) aims to help "older persons live with dignity in Canada and around the world." It delivers several programs to older people so that they can keep engaged with family and friends around the world. These courses also ensure that they can make the most of what technology can offer, helping them to participate fully in society.

Explor.ai (https://explor.ai/en) offers AI coaching for companies and individuals of all ages, including seniors, as well as coaching for developers. This will ensure that you will develop exactly what the market demands, thereby reducing costs.

United Kingdom

UK-based **Silver Sircle** (www.silversircle.com/services) gives technology support to families so that they are kept connected. If you have difficulty with technology-related issues, you can call the organization by subscribing to a range of packages.

Silver Sircle also gives recommendations regarding the gadgets that best help a person when it comes to health technology. These include technologies related to such problems as dementia and social isolation. In either case, robot companions may help and Silver Sircle will give advice on that. You can get in touch directly via support@silversircle.com.

British Institute of Learning Disabilities (BILD) (www. bild.org.uk) is based in the Institute of Research and Development in Birmingham, located next to the Queen Elizabeth Teaching Hospital. It gives positive support for people with disabilities, offering membership, conferences and training opportunities, particularly in the areas of positive thinking and communication. You can get in touch via enquiries@bild.org.uk.

Koenig Solutions is also available in the UK. For details of all the courses on offer, go to www.koenig-solutions.com or get in touch directly via info@koenig-solutions.com.

Age UK (www.ageuk.org.uk), which is the country's largest charity dedicated to helping everyone make the most of later life, offers digital training for older people. It aims to increase their skills and confidence. There's a loan plan so that those who don't have access to a particular technology, whether it is a laptop computer or tablet, can borrow what they need.

There are no set lesson plans. The learners are encouraged to pick their own topics and these topics can be repeated as many times as needed.

Age UK says it helps more than 5 million older people every year by providing support, companionship and advice. The Age UK network includes Age Cymru, Age Northern Ireland and Age Scotland and around 165 local Age UK partners in England.

You can also get information about the latest products for seniors including insurance, funeral plans, legal services, incontinence products, personal alarms and bathing equipment. Go to www.ageco.co.uk for contact details.

Alpha Training (www.alphatraining.com/services) offers training at all levels on IT as well as leadership and management, and personal effectiveness. Courses are delivered either in a classroom environment, through one-to-one coaching or via presentations to organizations and individuals. The courses on IT that are available cover Microsoft, Adobe, Google and various apps, including Zoom, Trello and Slack. Get in touch via +44 (0)20 8658 6994.

Advantages of Age (AOA) (https://advantagesofage.com/exclusives/over-50-want-to-set-up-your-own-business-startup-school-for-seniors-is-for-you) helps over-fifties to access a pro-aging community of like-minded people. Funded by local authorities, trusts and foundations, its eight-week course has been designed for anyone over fifty who is unemployed and wants to run a business, but doesn't know where to start. Part of this training is dedicated to technical updates and modern methods of operating in the business world. AOA firmly believes that those over fifty, sixty and even seventy can carry on working, no matter their starting position, and compete in the marketplace.

Catalyst IT Europe (www.catalyst-eu.net) is based in Brighton and provides in-house training on open sourcing solutions for businesses. Get in touch via+44 (0) 1273 929450.

Nesta UK is an innovation foundation for social good and is based in London. The organization acts through a combination of programs, investment, policy and research, and the formation of partnerships across a broad range of sectors, including teaming up with Codecademy to offer coding training. To learn more about the courses that are available, many of which are online, go to www.nesta.org.uk.

Rest Less UK (www.restless.co.uk) is for the over-fifties. It focuses on such issues as careers, finance, learning, volunteering and lifestyle.

New Zealand

SeniorNet (https://seniornet.nz) connects seniors with technology. It's a membership organization and the courses are made available locally at a community center. Workshops are also available. On its website, there are several online courses that allow seniors to get up to speed with technology including: "Learning more about your device", "Better online presentation skills", "Social media and networking", "Confidence online", "Online banking and insurance", "Buying and selling online", "Organizing your photos and documents", "Keeping safe online", "Creating and delivering publications and presentations", "Making photo books".

Wavelength (https://wavelength.co.nz/portfolio) provides online digital training for all age groups. It has offices in Wellington, Auckland and Sydney, Australia.

Synapsys (www.synapsys.co.nz/services) is a digital-training company based in Wellington. It provides training for all age groups, but is focused on providing in-house solutions for businesses rather than for individuals. Get in touch via 04 801 8478.

Catalyst Training (www.catalyst.net.nz) offers workshops for a range of ages to bring them up to speed with different technologies. There are offices across New Zealand, Australia and Europe.

Koenig Solutions is also available in New Zealand. For details of all the courses on offer, go to www.koenig-solutions.com or get in touch via info@koenig-solutions.com or +99 10710143.

Age Concern NZ promotes wellbeing, rights as well as respect and dignity for older people. It makes special reference to older people in Māori communities, koroua and kuia. The principles it focuses on are:

- Dignity—to respect the dignity and uniqueness of every person as an individual and as a valuable member of society.

- Wellbeing—to ensure that older people are given the opportunities to achieve physical comfort, engage in satisfying activities and personal development, and feel valued and supported.

- Equity—to ensure that older people have an equal opportunity to achieve wellbeing by directing resources to help those disadvantaged or in greatest need.

- Cultural respect—to respect the values and social structures of Māori and people of other cultural and ethnic backgrounds, demonstrating this by working together to gain mutual understanding.

For more information go to www.ageconcern.org.nz.

Australia

Age Concern Australia was established in 1986 and is one of Australia's oldest continuing private professional development organizations for registered enrolled nurses, and now nurse practitioners. It empowers nurses, allied health professionals and other healthcare workers through evidence-based education and training. Its vision is to set the standard of excellence in education and training in gerontic care, thereby enhancing the quality-of-care outcomes for all older Australians. For more information go to https://ageconcern.com.au.

Non-technology-related support

Seniors need different types of support at different times and as they age, a certain kind of support is needed. It may be that people just want someone with whom they can socialize, whether that is with an individual, through a dating agency (online or offline) or in a social club. It may be that they have a disease, such as cancer or dementia, or an addiction. In some cases, people may have had support when they were younger and this needs to continue as they age.

Different societies have different types of support groups and charities. It is up to each person to research where best to get the support they need. Some charities offer emotional support and others practical support, but they all help older people age with dignity.

Although joining a support group can be helpful, sometimes people just want someone to talk to and socialize with. Whether you are living on your own in your own home or in a retirement village, there are many activities in which you can engage, such as bowls, croquet, bridge and other card games, or pickleball. Some support groups will help when it comes to elections, including with voter registration and providing transport to an election and other civic engagement events.

Across most societies, there tend to be seven types of support group:

Chronic condition/illness support group

This type of support exists for people over sixty who suffer from some type of disease or illness. Maybe it is cancer or diabetes, or deafness, or heart problems, or stroke, or loneliness. In these cases, people frequently need help and support—emotional and practical—including:

- Support from older adults with the same condition
- Tips for effective daily management
- Access to reliable information about supplemental treatments
- Regular visits by a nurse or home carer if appropriate
- Meals delivered to the home regularly

Grief support groups

These groups give support to people who are adjusting to life without their partner, loved one or anyone close. Sometimes, grief becomes harder to bear the older you get. Grieving rarely seems to get any easier.

There are a number of places offering grief support such as local senior citizen centers, churches, funeral homes, hospitals and clinics. These places often act as a supplement to the support given by family members. It might also be appropriate to access home carers or counselors.

Dementia-related support groups

Seniors diagnosed with dementia, whether onset or early stages, may benefit from support groups for older adults. So too may family members or caregivers. There is probably a local support group near you.

Alzheimer's is one of the most common forms of dementia. Different support groups are available for this and other forms of dementia, and they help by:

- Addressing the many emotions that go along with a dementia diagnosis

- Providing access to credible new research

- Offering recommendations for activities or therapies that could slow dementia progression

- Giving both seniors and family caregivers a way to discuss feelings and concerns

Addiction recovery support groups

Addiction plagues people of all ages. Once seniors have received appropriate treatment for addiction, support groups can help them remain focused on their recovery moving forward. It may be that these groups recommend techniques and activities seniors can explore to remain relaxed and focused post-treatment or give older members easy access to additional assistance should there be setbacks or unexpected challenges.

Support groups to help with lifestyle changes

It's not unusual for seniors to face difficulties with efforts to stop smoking, shed unwanted pounds, eat well or stick to exercise routines, especially if they find it hard to walk. Sometimes, a local or national association has a quit-smoking action plan and/or a weight-loss campaign.

Some local gyms offer exercise groups for older members, as do some senior centers, so do some research to find a gym in your area that provides resources for older adults. Joining a gym or support group often provides an added incentive to stay motivated and achieve personal goals.

Support groups that provide practical help

Some support groups or charities, such as Age UK or Age Concern NZ, can provide part-time carers or assistants as well as meals to seniors if required (this service is called Meals on Wheels in some countries, such as the UK or New Zealand). They may also conduct classes in Pilates or yoga, or even technology. If they don't offer these themselves, they can usually point you in the right direction to find them.

Learning

Retirement is an opportunity to learn new subjects like languages or to brush up on old skills, such as managing personal finances. You may even learn more about how to use the latest technology. There are many free online courses available through platforms such as Coursera. Your public library, Citizens' Advice Bureau (or the equivalent) and support groups or charities that deal with the elderly will have the most up-to-date information on what is available.

Older people may choose to be involved in conferences on aging to learn more about this subject as well as related ones, perhaps becoming advocates for seniors as a result. A quick search of the internet using key words such as "aging" and "conference" will let you know what is available at any particular time.

References

Introduction

1   Jones, R. "UK state pension age may rise to 68 in 2030s, reports say – what is going on?" (*The Guardian*, 2023) www.theguardian.com/money/2023/jan/25/uk-state-pension-age-rise-68

2   "New Zealand superannuation" (Work and Income Te Hiranga Tangata, nd) www.workandincome.govt.nz/products/a-z-benefits/nz-superannuation.html

3   "Retirement plans in the USA" (The American Dream, nd) www.the-american-dream.com/retirement-plan-usa

4   Schonfeld, E. "Interview with Senate candidate Carly Fiorina: 'The nation with the best brain power wins'" (*TechCrunch*, 2010) https://techcrunch.com/2010/01/31/interview-carly-fiorina-senate

PART ONE—Common Concerns About Technology

Chapter 1: What Are All These Technologies?

1   "Artificial Intelligence" (Wikipedia, nd) https://en.wikipedia.org/wiki/Artificial_intelligence and "How AI really works" (AI Transparency Institute, 2021) https://aitransparencyinstitute.com/what-is-ai

2   Anyoha, R. "The history of artificial intelligence" (Science in the News, 2017) www.sitn.harvard.edu/flash/2017/history-artificial-intelligence

3   Stevenson, A. (Editor) *Oxford Dictionary of English* (Oxford University Press, third edition 2010)

4   Seifert D. "Say hello to Astro, Alexa on Wheels" (*The Verge*, 2021) www.theverge.com/2021/9/28/22697244/amazon-astro-home-robot-hands-on-features-price

5   Joshi, A. "Win the fourth industrial revolution with artificial intelligence" (IBM, 2021) www.ibm.com/blogs/journey-to-ai/2021/04/win-the-fourth-industrial-revolution-with-artificial-intelligence and Matthews, K. "IoT and AI Tech: The backbone of the fourth industrial revolution" (*IoT Magazine*, 2020) https://theiotmagazine.com/iot-and-ai-tech-the-backbone-of-the-fourth-industrial-revolution-e7c6072fe1a9

6   Joshi, N. "7 types of artificial intelligence" (*Forbes*, 2019) www.
forbes.com/sites/cognitiveworld/2019/06/19/7-types-of-artificial-
intelligence/?sh=caec9dc233ee

7   Ibid

8   Ibid

9   Ibid

10   Ibid

11   "What is artificial intelligence and how is it used?" (News, European
Parliament, 2021) www.europarl.europa.eu/news/en/headlines/
society/20200827STO85804/what-is-artificial-intelligence-and-how-is-it-used

12   "Free Guy" (20th Century Studios, 2021) www.20thcenturystudios.com/
movies/free-guy

13   World Economic Forum "By 2030, AI will contribute $15 trillion to the
global economy" (weforum.org, 2019) www.weforum.org/agenda/2019/08/by-
2030-ai-will-contribute-15-trillion-to-the-global-economy

14   Morgan, B. "How Amazon has reorganized around artificial
intelligence and machine learning" (*Forbes*, 2018) www.forbes.com/sites/
blakemorgan/2018/07/16/how-amazon-has-re-organized-around-artificial-
intelligence-and-machine-learning/?sh=2efdf2197361

15   Bourke, J. "Amazon brings its till-free grocery store brand to Dalston"
(*Evening Standard*, 8 September 2021) www.standard.co.uk/business/leisure-
retail/amazon-brings-its-tillfree-grocery-store-brand-to-dalston-b954219.html

16   Zwieglinska, Z. "Stylist Gemma Sheppard is the first metaverse global
fashion director" (*Glossy*, 2022) www.glossy.co/fashion/gemma-sheppard-is-the-
first-metaverse-global-fashion-director

17   Jackson, L.M. "Shudu Gram is a white man's digital projection of real-
life black womanhood" (*The New Yorker*, 2018) www.newyorker.com/culture/
culture-desk/shudu-gram-is-a-white-mans-digital-projection-of-real-life-black-
womanhood

18   Klein, M. "The problematic fakery of Lil Miquela explained—An
exploration of virtual influencers and realness" (*Forbes*, 2020) www.forbes.com/
sites/mattklein/2020/11/17/the-problematic-fakery-of-lil-miquela-explained-
an-exploration-of-virtual-influencers-and-realness/?sh=185d3bc61b8d

19   Lamerichs, N. "Lil Miquela, Lightning and other virtual influencers"
(Nicolle Lamerichs, 2018) https://nicollelamerichs.com/2018/10/15/lil-
miquela-lightning-and-other-virtual-influencers

20   Iglhaut, C. "The influencers of tomorrow will be virtual" (deutschland.de, 2019) www.deutschland.de/en/topic/culture/who-is-noonoouri-fashion-avatar-conquers-the-fashion-world

21   "The environmental cost of fashion" (Geneva Environment Network, nd) www.genevaenvironmentnetwork.org/resources/updates/sustainable-fashion

22   "UN Alliance for Sustainable Fashion addresses damage of 'fast fashion'" (UN Environment Programme, nd) www.unep.org/news-and-stories/press-release/un-alliance-sustainable-fashion-addresses-damage-fast-fashion

23   Gosselin, V. "How artificial intelligence can help fashion brands be more sustainable" (Heuritech, 2019) www.heuritech.com/articles/fashion-solutions/how-artificial-intelligence-can-help-fashion-brands-be-more-sustainable

24   Sharma, D. "5 AI-powered startups revolutionizing fashion industry" (*Analytics Vidhya*, 2002) www.analyticsvidhya.com/blog/2022/08/5-ai-powered-startups-revolutionizing-fashion-industry

25   www.stylumia.ai

26   McKay, R. "A bus that speaks sign language? Meet Olli" (IBM, 2018) www.ibm.com/blogs/industries/olli-ai-and-iot-autonomous-bus

27   "Testing autonomous transport" (Marineterrein Amsterdam, nd) www.marineterrein.nl/en/project/meet-olli-the-self-driving-minibus

28   Ryan, P. "Abu Dhabi's Masdar City launches self-driving shuttle service" (View from London, 2018) www.thenationalnews.com/uae/abu-dhabi-s-masdar-city-launches-self-driving-shuttle-service-1.783230

29   Pass notes "Tamagotchi kids: Could the future of parenthood be having virtual children in the metaverse?" (*The Guardian*, 2022) www.theguardian.com/technology/2022/may/31/tamagotchi-kids-future-parenthood-virutal-children-metaverse

30   Ibid

31   "Nokia CEO in Davos: By 2030, smartphones will not exist, technology 'built directly into our bodies'" (Rair Foundation, 2022) https://noqreport.com/2022/05/29/nokia-ceo-in-davos-by-2030-smartphones-will-not-exist-technology-built-directly-into-our-bodies-video

Chapter 2: Is Technology Desirable?

1   Leslie, D. "Understanding artificial intelligence ethics and safety: A guide for the responsible design and implementation of AI systems in the public

sector" (The Alan Turing Institute, 2019) www.turing.ac.uk/sites/default/
files/2019-08/understanding_artificial_intelligence_ethics_and_safety.pdf

2   "Public Relations Ethics Training" (The Arthur W. Page Center, nd)
www.pagecentertraining.psu.edu

3   Duong, M. "How to know if your phone is being tracked. Check this!"
(TechUntold, 2023) www.techuntold.com/how-to-know-your-phone-being-
tracked

4   Balasaygun, K. "The new iPhone 14 and iOS upgrade include some big
cybersecurity changes" (*CNBC*, 2022) www.cnbc.com/2022/11/25/buying-new-
iphone-here-are-new-features-designed-for-your-security.html and Kastranekes,
J. "Pixel 4 Recorder app can transcribe speech in real time without an internet
connection" (*The Verge*, 2019) www.theverge.com/2019/10/15/20915452

5   McElhearn, K. and Long J. "Apple AirTags: The complete guide to how
they work, what to track with them, and more" (Intego, 2022) www.intego.com/
mac-security-blog/complete-guide-to-apple-airtags-how-to-use-them-how-they-
work-and-what-to-track-with-them

6   "An update on AirTag and unwanted tracking" (Apple.com, 2022)
www.apple.com/uk/newsroom/2022/02/an-update-on-airtag-and-unwanted-
tracking

7   Kastrenakes, J. "Pixel 4 Recorder app can transcribe speech in real
time without an internet connection" (The Verge, 2019) www.theverge.
com/2019/10/15/20915452/google-pixel-4-recorder-app-transcription-real-
time-free-language-processing

8   Hitrova, C. "The Alan Turing Institute publishes a comprehensive guide
for the responsible design and implementation of AI systems in the public
sector" (European AI Alliance, 2019) https://futurium.ec.europa.eu/en/
european-ai-alliance/document/alan-turing-institute-publishes-comprehensive-
guide-responsible-design-and-implementation-ai-systems?language=en

9   Ibid

10   Capgemini press release "Organizations must proactively address ethics
in AI to gain the public's trust and loyalty" (Capgemini, 2019) www.capgemini.
com/wp-content/uploads/2019/07/2019_07_05_Press-Release_Ethics-in-
AI-_EN.pdf

11   "Artificial intelligence and ethics: The fundamentals every organizational
leader should consider when embracing AI" (The SAS AI ethics primer, 2019)
www.sas.com/en/whitepapers/artificial-intelligence-and-ethics-111452.html

12   Whitepaper "AI and Empathy: Combining artificial intelligence with human ethics for better engagement" (Pega, 2019) www.pega.com/insights/resources/ai-and-empathy-combining-artificial-intelligence-human-ethics-better-engagement

13   Ibid

14   Manasi, A., Panchanadeswaran, S., Sours, E., and Lee, SJ. "Mirroring the bias: gender and artificial intelligence" (*Gender, Technology, and Development*, 2022, 26:3, 295-305) www.tandfonline.com/doi/full/10.1080/09718524.2022.2128254

15   Botha, M. "The limits of artificial intelligence" (*Towards Data Science*, 2019) https://towardsdatascience.com/the-limits-of-artificial-intelligence-fdcc78bf263b

16   Yeruva, V. "Autonomous vehicles and their impact on the economy" (Forbes, 2022) www.forbes.com/sites/forbestechcouncil/2022/02/14/autonomous-vehicles-and-their-impact-on-the-economy

17   Crawford, K. *Atlas of AI: Power, politics, and the planetary costs of artificial intelligence* (Yale University Press, 2022)

18   Ibid

Chapter 3: What If I Get It Wrong?

1   Mike Collins interview, April 12 2022

2   Malik, D. "Study: 78 percent people forget their passwords and then go for reset!" (*Digital Information World*, 2019) www.digitalinformationworld.com/2019/12/new-password-study-finds-78-of-people-had-to-reset-a-password-they-forgot-in-past-90-days.html

3   Hutson, M. "Artificial intelligence just made guessing your password a whole lot easier" (Science, 2017) www.science.org/content/article/artificial-intelligence-just-made-guessing-your-password-whole-lot-easier

4   Averre, D. "End of the line: Plans for ALL rail ticket offices are to close as sales go online despite fears 3 million over-65s who don't have internet access" (*MailOnline*, 2022) www.dailymail.co.uk/news/article-10931017/End-line-railway-ticket-offices-sales-online.html

5   Ibid

6   Fritscher, L. "What is fear?" (Very Well Mind, updated 2022) www.verywellmind.com/the-psychology-of-fear-2671696

7   "Technophobia" (Cleveland Clinic, last reviewed 2022) https://my.clevelandclinic.org/health/diseases/22853-technophobia

8   Bronston, B. "Study examines why the memory of fear is seared into our brains" (*Science Daily*, 2022) www.sciencedaily.com/releases/2022/06/220601133030.htm

9   "How can you be free from all fears with self-realization?" (Dadabhagwan.org, nd) www.dadabhagwan.org/path-to-happiness/spiritual-science/ways-to-overcome-fear/free-from-all-fears-with-self-realization

10   Elizabeth Blackwell Institute for Health Research, "Discovery of novel brain fear mechanisms offers target for anxiety-reducing drugs" (University of Bristol, 2022) www.bristol.ac.uk/blackwell/news/2022/neuroscience-fear-pathways.html

11   "Discovery of novel brain fear mechanisms offers target for anxiety-reducing drugs" (University of Bristol, 2022) www.bristol.ac.uk/blackwell/news/2022/neuroscience-fear-pathways.html

12   "Overcoming the fear of technology" (ClassCover, 2020) www.classcover.com.au/blog/overcoming-the-fear-of-technology

13   "How technology use affects the spine" (Rothman Orthopedics, 2019) https://rothmanortho.com/stories/blog/how-computer-and-smart-phone-use-affect-the-spine

14   Alcover, C-M. et al. "'Aging-and-tech job vulnerability': A proposed framework on the dual impact of aging and AI, robotics, and automation among older workers" (Organizational Psychology Review 11: 2, 2021) https://journals.sagepub.com/doi/abs/10.1177/2041386621992105

15   Ibid

16   Ibid

17   Written by Anne Mayer Bird exclusively for *SeniorITy*

18   Mayer, C. and Mayer Bird, A. *Good Grief: Embracing life at the time of death* (HarperCollins, 2021)

PART TWO —Taking Control Of Technology

1   Roser, M., Ortiz-Ospina, E., Ritchie, H. "Life expectancy" (Our World in Data, 2019) https://ourworldindata.org/life-expectancy

2   Heidegger, M. *The Question Concerning Technology and Other Essays* (HarperPerennial, 1982)

3   "Ageing" (United Nations, nd) www.un.org/en/global-issues/ageing

Chapter 4: Technology, Health And Safety

1   "Why Apple Watch? It's the ultimate device for a healthy life" (Apple, nd) www.apple.com/uk/watch/why-apple-watch

2   "How technology use affects the spine" (Rothman Orthopedics, 2019) https://rothmanortho.com/stories/blog/how-computer-and-smart-phone-use-affect-the-spine

3   Fitch, A. "Could AI keep people 'alive' after death?" (*Wall Street Journal*, 2021) www.wsj.com/articles/could-ai-keep-people-alive-after-death-11625317200

4   Pollak, S. "A new mourning: Grief in the digital age" (*The Irish Times*, 2014) www.irishtimes.com/life-and-style/people/a-new-mourning-grief-in-the-digital-age-1.1941728

5   Van Erp, M. et al. "Using natural language processing and artificial intelligence to explore the nutrition and sustainability of recipes and Food" (*Frontiers in Artificial Intelligence*, 2021) www.frontiersin.org/articles/10.3389/frai.2020.621577/full

6   Sharf, Z. "Val Kilmer recreated his speaking voice using artificial intelligence and hours of old audio" (*IndieWire*, 2021) www.indiewire.com/2021/08/val-kilmer-recreated-speaking-voice-ai-algorithm-1234658600 and Flynn, J. "Helping actor Val Kilmer reclaim his voice" (Sonantic, 2021) www.sonantic.io/blog/helping-actor-val-kilmer-reclaim-his-voice

7   Chung, A. "Innovative glasses uses AI to describe surroundings to blind and visually-impaired people in real time" (*The Sized*, 2022) www.thesized.com/envision-glasses-ai-describe-surroundings-blind-visually-impaired-people-in-real-time

8   "Innovation and new technology to help reduce NHS waiting lists" (GOV. UK, 2021) www.gov.uk/government/news/innovation-and-new-technology-to-help-reduce-nhs-waiting-lists and "Doctors beware: A 'robot' doctor just matched human's diagnostic performance" (Advisory Board, 2019) www.advisory.com/daily-briefing/2019/02/13/ai-diagnosis

9   Perraudin, F. "GP surgery closures in UK 'hit all-time high' in 2018" (*The Guardian*, 2019) www.theguardian.com/society/2019/may/31/gp-surgery-closures-in-uk-hit-all-time-high-in-2018

10   Industry Insights "5 ways energy data can help your business" (Chameleon Technology, 2018) https://chameleontechnology.co.uk/2018/07/09/5-ways-energy-data-can-help-your-business

11   Wright Stuff Inc. "Mind games: Playing games to prevent Alzheimer's" (ALZaids, 2016) www.alzaids.com/mind-games-playing-games-to-help-prevent-alzheimers

12   DeLuca, L.S. "How innovative technologies help an aging population stay healthier and happier" (IBM, 2018) www.ibm.com/blogs/internet-of-things/iot-ai-and-iot-help-an-aging-population

13   Ibid

14   Maderer, J. "Using the stairs just got easier with energy-recycling steps" (Georgia Tech, 2017) https://news.emory.edu/stories/2017/07/ting_energy_recycling_stairs/index.html

15   Ibid

16   Kooser, A. "Helmet-mounted crash sensor automatically calls for help" (*CNET*, 2012) www.cnet.com/culture/helmet-mounted-crash-sensor-automatically-calls-for-help

17   Knebl, A. "A robot with a gentle touch" (Max-Planck-Gesellschaft, 2022) www.mpg.de/18512185/haptics-robots-touch

18   Marr, B. "How robots, IoT and artificial intelligence are changing how humans have sex" (*Forbes*, 2019) www.forbes.com/sites/bernardmarr/2019/04/01/how-robots-iot-and-artificial-intelligence-are-changing-how-humans-have-sex/?sh=5c8b487e329c

19   Keach, S. "Smart sex toys get ALEXA upgrade: Your first threesome could be with an artificial intelligence" (*The Sun*, 2018) www.thesun.co.uk/tech/6825412/smart-sex-toy-alexa-lovense-vibrator

20   Bame, Y. "Sex with a robot? 1 in 4 men would consider it" (YouGovAmerica, 2017) https://today.yougov.com/topics/society/articles-reports/2017/10/02/1-4-men-would-consider-having-sex-robot

21   Richardson, K. "The asymmetrical 'relationship': Parallels between prostitution and the development of sex robots" (Campaign against Sex Robots, n.d.) https://campaignagainstsexrobots.org/papers

22   Duckworth, D., et al. "Therabot (TM): The initial design of a robotic therapy support system" www.researchgate.net/profile/Cindy-Bethel-2/publication/300906168_Therabot/links/586b34d108ae6eb871ba8fb0/Therabot.pdf

23   Paro, www.parorobots.com

24   Anyangwe, E. "This global public health challenge affects one in four women. Where's the outrage or the plan?" (*CNN Health*, 2022) https://edition.cnn.com/2022/02/17/health/intimate-partner-violence-lancet-as-equals-intl-cmd/index.html

25   "A third of women 'victims of domestic abuse'" (Sky News, 2014) https://news.sky.com/story/a-third-of-women-victims-of-domestic-abuse-10389529

26   Grogger, J., Ivandic, R., Kirchmaier, T. "Comparing conventional and machine-learning approaches to risk assessment in domestic abuse cases" (*Centre for Economic Performance*, 2020) https://ssrn.com/abstract=3532560

Chapter 5: Technology And Wealth

1   Kumar, S. "Use of artificial intelligence in banking world today" (*Finextra*, 2021) www.finextra.com/blogposting/20688/use-of-artificial-intelligence-in-banking-world-today

2   Harris, K. "Millions of Brits face being cut off from system as cash 'phased out in five years'" (*Daily Express*, 2022) www.express.co.uk/news/uk/1661639/cash-phased-out-five-years-banks-atm-cards-online-banking

3   "The Ministry is phasing out payment by cheque" (justice.govt.nz, nd) www.justice.govt.nz/about/news-and-media/news/the-ministry-is-phasing-out-payment-by-cheque

4   Harris, K. "Millions of Brits face being cut off from system as cash 'phased out in five years'" (*Daily Express*, 2022) www.express.co.uk/news/uk/1661639/cash-phased-out-five-years-banks-atm-cards-online-banking

5   "Nuance Gatekeeper" (Nuance, nd) www.nuance.com/omni-channel-customer-engagement/authentication-and-fraud-prevention/gatekeeper.html

6   "Nuance AI enables organizations to prioritize and protect seniors using the sound of their voice" (Nuance, 2020) https://news.nuance.com/2020-06-04-Nuance-AI-Enables-Organizations-to-Prioritize-and-Protect-Seniors-Using-the-Sound-of-Their-Voice

7   Ibid

8   Ibid

9   Newman, J. "This AI can guess your age from the sound of your voice" (*Fast Company*, 2020) www.fastcompany.com/90516397/this-ai-can-guess-your-age-from-the-sound-of-your-voice

10   "Online Banking, is it safe?" (Age UK, nd) www.ageuk.org.uk/
information-advice/work-learning/technology-internet/online-banking

11   Ibid

12   AARP and Age UK "Age-friendly banking: What it is and how you
do it" (Age UK and AARP, nd) www.ageuk.org.uk/globalassets/age-uk/
documents/reports-and-publications/reports-and-briefings/money-matters/
rb_april16_age_friendly_banking.pdf and Hill, A. "Banks must guarantee access
to cash for everyone, says Age UK" (*The Guardian*, 2021) www.theguardian.com/
business/2021/jun/26/banks-access-to-cash-age-uk-atms

13   Zelealem, F. "South Korea's KB Bank enters metaverse space" (Yahoo!
Finance, 2021) https://finance.yahoo.com/news/south-korea-kb-bank-
enters-121438920.html

14   Wells Fargo, www.wellsfargohistory.com/timeline-of-innovation

15   "Egg Banking – History" (liquisearch.com, nd) www.liquisearch.com/
egg_banking/history

16   Powers, J. "How AI trading technology is making stock market investors
smarter" (Built In, 2022) https://builtin.com/artificial-intelligence/ai-trading-
stock-market-tech

17   Specific research carried out by Natalie Lacazes Campbell, July 2001, for
and on behalf of Senior Behavioural Shift

18   McGregor, J. and Gray, L. "Stereotypes and older workers: The New
Zealand experience" (*Social Policy of New Zealand 18*, 2002) www.msd.govt.nz/
documents/about-msd-and-our-work/publications-resources/journals-and-
magazines/social-policy-journal/spj18/18-pages163-177.pdf

19   "Ageism is a global challenge: UN" (World Health Organization, 2021)
www.who.int/news/item/18-03-2021-ageism-is-a-global-challenge-un

20   "What will AI mean for older workers?" (Columbia: Mailman School of
Public Health, 2018) www.publichealth.columbia.edu/public-health-now/news/
what-will-ai-mean-older-workers

21   Ibid

22   Baxter, S. et al. "Is working in later life good for your health? A systematic
review of health outcomes resulting from extended working lives" (*BMC
Public Health* 21: 1356, 2021) https://bmcpublichealth.biomedcentral.com/
articles/10.1186/s12889-021-11423-2

Chapter 6: Technology And Day-To-Day Living

1   "Booklyn Co launches new AI-powered e-reader site" (Content Engine News Syndication, 2020) https://contentenginellc.com/2020/11/19/booklynco-launches-new-ai-powered-e-reader-site

2   Ibid

3   "Dyslexia" (British Dyslexia Association, nd) www.bdadyslexia.org.uk/dyslexia

4   "Dyslexia – the facts" (Develop Us, 2020) www.developus.wales/dyslexia-the-facts

5   Ibid

6   "12 famous people who struggled with dyslexia before changing the world" (IMSE Journal, 2017) https://journal.imse.com/12-famous-people-who-struggled-with-dyslexia-before-changing-the-world

7   Burns, J. "Radisson Blu Edwardian guests can now text Edward the chatbot for service" (*Forbes*, 2016) www.forbes.com/sites/janetwburns/2016/05/10/radisson-blu-hotel-guests-can-now-text-edward-the-chatbot-for-service/?sh=67ab9b771e23 and "Edwardian Hotels London launches 'virtual host' designed by Aspect Software" (*Businesswire*, 2016) www.businesswire.com/news/home/20160509005368/en/Edwardian-Hotels-London-Launches-%E2%80%98Virtual-Host%E2%80%99-Designed

8   "Hilton Worldwide: LightStay" (Environment and Energy Leader, nd) www.environmentalleader.com/products/hilton-worldwide-lightstay and "LightStay – A decade of managing our environmental and social impact" (Hilton.com, 2019) https://stories.hilton.com/hilton-history/lightstay-a-decade-of-managing-our-environmental-and-social-impact

9   "Olli debuts in Italy: Turin deploys the 3D-printed driverless shuttle" (2020) www.sustainable-bus.com/its/olli-debuts-in-italy-turin-deploys-the-3d-printed-driverless-shuttle

10   Ryan, P. "Abu Dhabi's Masdar City launches self-driving shuttle service" (View from London, 2018) www.thenationalnews.com/uae/abu-dhabi-s-masdar-city-launches-self-driving-shuttle-service-1.783230

11   "Masdar City welcomes world's first AI university" (Masdar, 2019) https://news.masdar.ae/en/news/2019/10/23/09/46/masdar-city-welcomesworlds-first-ai-university

12   Bourke, J. "Amazon brings its till-free grocery store brand to Dalston" (Evening Standard, 8 September 2021) www.standard.co.uk/business/ leisureretail/amazon-brings-its-tillfree-grocery-store-brand-to-dalston-b954219. html

13   "The top 10 best fashion software tools for apparel brands in 2022" (WFX, 2022) www.worldfashionexchange.com/blog/the-top-fashion-software-tools-for-apparel-brands

14   O'Hear, S. "Virtual fitting startup Virtusize tries on Japan via partnership with online fashion retailer Magaseek" (*TechCrunch*, 2013) https://techcrunch. com/2013/08/20/virtusize-tries-on-japan

15   Marain, A. translated by Green, S. "From Lil Miquela to Shudu Gram: Meet the virtual models" (*Vogue*, 2019) www.vogue.fr/fashion/ fashion-inspiration/story/from-lil-miquela-to-shudu-gram-meet-the-virtual-models/1843

16   Ibid

17   Toureille, C. "TV fashion guru Gemma Sheppard becomes the first stylist to enter the Metaverse where she'll charge real money to style virtual avatars" (*Daily Mail*, 2022) www.dailymail.co.uk/femail/article-10422827/10-Years-Younger-10-Days-Gemma-Sheppard-worlds-stylist-enter-Metaverse.html

18   "Safely monitor your elderly parents with their consent" (SeniorSafetyApp.com, nd) www.seniorsafetyapp.com/safely-monitor-your-elderly-parents-with-their-consent/

19   "Tommy Hilfiger smart clothes track wearers" (*BBC News*, 2018) www.bbc.com/news/technology-44965150 and "Ralph Lauren introduces the next evolution of wearable technology" (Global Brands, nd) www. globalbrandsmagazine.com/ralph-lauren-introduces-he-next-evolution-of-wearable-technology

20   GrandPad "Key factors in making technology work for seniors" (GrandPad, 2020) https://static1.squarespace.com/ static/5d30eb93b1af2d00015a4bd0/t/5fdcf5f3f3c4297b02d32a39/1608316406 421/0130+Key+factors+in+making+technology+work+for+seniors.pdf

21   Kroll, M. "Prolonged social isolation and loneliness are equivalent to smoking 15 cigarettes a day" (University of New Hampshire, 2022) https:// extension.unh.edu/blog/2022/05/prolonged-social-isolation-loneliness-are-equivalent-smoking-15-cigarettes-day

PART THREE —The Future Of Seniors

Chapter 7: Ways Technology Can Enhance The Life Of Seniors

1   Akinola, S. "What is the biggest benefit technology will have on ageing and longevity?" (World Economic Forum, 2021) www.weforum.org/agenda/2021/03/what-is-the-biggest-benefit-technology-ageing-longevity-global-future-council-tech-for-good

2   "Tech usage among older adults skyrockets during pandemic" (AARP, 2021) https://press.aarp.org/2021-4-21-Tech-Usage-Among-Older-Adults-Skyrockets-During-Pandemic

3   Kakulla, B. "Personal tech and the pandemic: Older adults are upgrading for a better online experience" (AARP, 2021) www.aarp.org/research/topics/technology/info-2021/2021-technology-trends-older-americans.html

4   "Ensuring artificial intelligence technologies for health benefit older people" (World Health Organization, 2022) www.who.int/news/item/09-02-2022-ensuring-artificial-intelligence-%28ai%29-technologies-for-health-benefit-older-people

5   Adams, N., Stubbs, D., Woods, V. "Psychological barriers to internet usage among older adults in the UK" (Robens Centre for Health Ergonomics) www.semanticscholar.org/paper/Psychological-barriers-to-Internet-usage-among-in-Adams-Stubbs/afe94f87cc97642c10a44fadc423fbea9d150282

6   Smith, A. and Anderson, M. "Automation in Everyday life" (Pew Research Center, 2017) www.pewresearch.org/internet/2017/10/04/automation-in-everyday-life

7   Standage, T. "Automation and anxiety: Will smarter machines cause mass unemployment?" (*The Economist*, 2016) www.economist.com/special-report/2016/06/23/automation-and-anxiety

8   "September 2, 1969: First ATM opens" (History 101, 2023) https://history101.com/september-2-1969-first-atm-opens

9   "New job opportunities in an ageing society" (ILO, 2019) www.ilo.org/global/about-the-ilo/how-the-ilo-works/multilateral-system/g20/reports/WCMS_713372/lang--en/index.htm

10   "Older workers' outdated skills and resistance to retraining" (The Centre for Research Into The Older Workforce, nd) www.agediversity.org/course/older-workers-outdated-skills-and-resistance-to-retraining

11   Harasty, C. and Ostermeier, M. "Population ageing: Alternative measure of dependency and implications for the future of work" (ILO, 2020) www.ilo.org/global/publications/working-papers/WCMS_747257/lang--en/index.htm

12   Ibid

Chapter 8: What's Next For Technology?

1   Clemente, J. "Financial services: Trustworthy AI's promise and payoff"(IBM, 2021) www.ibm.com/blogs/journey-to-ai/2021/07/financial-services-can-win-with-ai-by-putting-trust-first

2   "SAE J3016 levels of driving automation" (SAE, nd) www.sae.org/binaries/content/assets/cm/content/blog/sae-j3016-visual-chart_5.3.21.pdf

3   Blanco, S. "BMW Level 3 autonomous driving tech is coming in 2025" (*Car and Driver*, 2022) www.caranddriver.com/news/a39414801/bmw-autonomous-driving-tech-2025

4   Blanco, S. "Driverless cars could reduce traffic fatalities by up to 90%, says report" (*Car and Driver*, 2022) www.caranddriver.com/news/a39414801/bmw-autonomous-driving-tech-2025

5   Hall, H. "The 10 largest chip manufacturers in the world and what they do" (History-Computer, 2022) https://history-computer.com/the-10-largest-chip-manufacturers-in-the-world-and-what-they-do

6   Lapedus, M. "In-memory vs near-memory computing" (*Semiconductor Engineering*, 2019) https://semiengineering.com/in-memory-vs-near-memory-computing

7   Fleischman, T. "Technology helps self-driving cars learn from own memories" (*Cornell Chronicle*, 2022) https://news.cornell.edu/stories/2022/06/technology-helps-self-driving-cars-learn-own-memories

8   Poonia, G. "Unlocking digital fashion: Clothes for your online self" (*Deseret News*, 2022) www.deseret.com/2022/1/27/22859139/digital-fashion-video-game-metaverse-nike-adidas-gucci-fabricant-dressx

9   "Metaverse NFT that will grow in value in 2022" (EFT, 2021) https://etfhead.com/metaverse-nft-that-will-grow-in-value-in-2022

10   Ibid

11   "Digital signature market worth $25.2 billion by 2027 – Exclusive report by MarketsandMarkets" (Cision, 2022) https://www.prnewswire.com/news-releases/digital-signature-market-worth-25-2-billion-by-2027---exclusive-report-by-marketsandmarkets-301656848.html

12   "What is artificial intelligence?" (NICE, nd) https://au.nice.com/glossary/what-is-contact-center-ai-artificial-intelligence

13   Savage, M. "Thousands of Swedes are inserting microchips under their skin" (*NPR*, 2018) www.npr.org/2018/10/22/658808705/thousands-of-swedes-are-inserting-microchips-under-their-skin

14   "Shiseido virtual skin analysis" (Shiseido, nd) www.shiseido.co.uk/gb/en/virtual-skincare-consultation.html

15   Jiraittiwanna, T. "How Burberry promotes its brand through WeChat in China (LinkedIn, 2019) www.linkedin.com/pulse/3-how-burberry-promotes-brand-through-wechat-china-jiraittiwanna

16   Henderson, E. "Deep Longevity and Human Longevity announce collaboration to deploy AI-powered aging clocks" (*News Medical Life Sciences*, 2020) www.news-medical.net/news/20200714/Deep-Longevity-and-Human-Longevity-announce-collaboration-to-deploy-AI-powered-aging-clocks.aspx

17   "Bryte restorative bed" (DesignWell, 2021) https://designwell365.com/products/seating-furniture/bryte-restorative-bed

18   "Eight Sleep Pod Mattress – Feel the 'technologically modified' sleep!" (Slumberly, 2023) https://slumberly.org/eight-sleep-mattress-review

19   PTI "AI that can identify sleep disorders developed by UK scientists" (*The Week*, 2021) www.theweek.in/news/sci-tech/2021/07/22/ai-that-can-identify-sleep-disorders-developed-by-uk-scientists.html

20   Ibid

21   O'Brien, S.A. and Yurieff, K. "7 startups that want to improve your mental health" (*CNN*, 2018) https://money.cnn.com/gallery/technology/2018/05/25/self-care-apps-mental-health/6.html

22   "The next generation bed alarm" (Toch Sleepsense, nd) www.tochsleepsense.com

23   Yamada, K. "CarePredict Home: The wearable for the elderly that can save a life" (MUO, 2020) www.makeuseof.com/tag/carepredict-home-wearable-elderly-can-save-life

24   "Get the facts on falls prevention"(National Council on Aging (NCoA), 2022) www.ncoa.org/article/get-the-facts-on-falls-prevention

25   Staff Reporters "DOOH development accelerates in Singapore and Hong Kong with key partnerships" (*Campaign*, 2021) www.campaignasia.com/article/dooh-development-accelerates-in-singapore-and-hong-kong-with-key-partnerships/471223

Chapter 9: How Technology Affects Body Language

1   Vischer, A. "The best posture correctors to help your working from home back pain (as seen on Strictly)" (*Grazia*, 2022) https://graziadaily.co.uk/beauty-hair/skin/best-posture-correctors-back-braces

2   "HKUST scientists develop world's first spherical artificial eye with 3D retina" (Hong Kong University of Science and Technology, 2020) https://news.hkust.edu.hk/news/hkust-scientists-develop-worlds-first-spherical-artificial-eye-3d-retina

3   "Axonify acquires Nudge to bring digital employee experience to the next level" (Press Release, 2022) https://axonify.com/en-uk/news/axonify-acquires-nudge-to-bring-digital-employee-experience-to-the-next-level

4   "Facial recognition market size, share & trends analysis report by technology (2D, 3D, facial analytics), by application (access control, security & surveillance), by end-use, by region, and segment forecasts, 2021–2028" (GrandView Research, 2020) www.grandviewresearch.com/industry-analysis/facial-recognition-market

5   Rasmussen, M. "How avatars transformed the internet" (Virtual Humans, 2021) www.virtualhumans.org/article/how-avatars-transformed-the-internet

6   Nellis, S. "Nvidia doubles down on software tools for crafting virtual worlds" (*Reuters*, 2021) www.reuters.com/technology/nvidia-doubles-down-software-tools-crafting-virtual-worlds-2021-11-09

Conclusion

1   "World population will increase by 2.5 billion 2050; people over 60 to increase by more than 1 billion" (UN, 2007) https://press.un.org/en/2007/pop952.doc.htm

2   Boyd, C. "The changing face of ageing Britain: Fascinating charts and maps show how over-65s now outnumber under-15s for first time EVER, women dwarf men in all but 13 council areas and there are 300,000 fewer children under age of four compared to 2011" (*MailOnline*, 2022) www.dailymail.co.uk/health/article-10964321/Census-2021-changing-face-ageing-Britain-65s-outnumber-15s-women-dwarf-men.html

3   "World Population Prospects, 2019: Highlights" (UN, 2019) https://population.un.org/wpp/publications/files/wpp2019_highlights.pdf

4   "Aging and health" (World Health Organization, 2022) www.who.int/news-room/fact-sheets/detail/ageing-and-health

5   "Nokia CEO in Davos: By 2030, smartphones will not exist, technology 'built directly into our bodies'" (Rair Foundation, 2022) https://noqreport. com/2022/05/29/nokia-ceo-in-davos-by-2030-smartphones-will-not-exist-technology-built-directly-into-our-bodies-video

The Authors

1   Railton, C. *The Future of Body Language: How to communicate effectively through multimedia* (Hothive Books, 2010)

2   Railton, C. *Personal Branding* www.thebcfgroup.co.uk/training-and-development-ebooks/index.php

Acknowledgments

We would like to thank everyone who provided ideas and input for this book from all over the world. We would especially like to thank those we interviewed.

Carole would like to acknowledge Dee, Tanya and Jack who work at the TIN Café in London E8 for all the fun, teas and coffees they delivered.

The Authors

 **Lucia Dore** is a financial and business investigative journalist and editor with many years of experience in the print and online media. Working in the UK and Europe, the Middle East, Asia and Asia Pacific, she has written articles, white papers, management reports and books.

She co-founded Behavioural Shift with Carole Railton. The company looks at the interaction of people who are sixty-five and over with technology, aiming to empower the older person in the modern world.

She is also a researcher and communications professional. In 2015, she completed a documentary film entitled *Stepping Up: NZ's response to the refugee crisis* (www.luciadore.com/blog/stepping-up-nz-s-response-to-the-refugee-crisis). Lucia lives on the South Island of New Zealand where she can indulge her love of the outdoors and travel to different parts of the world.

You can connect with Lucia via:

🌐 www.behaviouralshift.com

🌐 www.luciadore.com

f Behavioural Shift

in www.linkedin.com/in/lucia-dore-23278

Carole Railton FRSA is a global body-language specialist whose interest in electronics began at the age of ten, soldering television tuners for pocket money on her parents' kitchen table. Initially, she worked for IBM in Zambia, then she returned to the UK and went on to work for DataPoint in the USA and UK, and Xerox in the UK and the Middle East, where her roles included training, sales management and directorships.

At twenty-three years old, Carole found out that she had a sister she'd never known about. In that moment, she vowed never to be lied to again and began learning about body language. Now in her seventies, she works as a global body-language consultant and keynote speaker with international organizations and business leaders, showing them how to communicate with clarity and impact using modern body-language behaviors. Ranked tenth in the world of global body-language consultants with experience in 47 countries, Carole has worked with KPMG Singapore, IBM France, Google London, CFEO Nigeria and recently a Thai university.

She has authored *The Future of Body Language*[1] and *A Useful Guide to Personal Branding*,[2] and appears regularly in international media. Carole is co-founder and director of Behavioural Shift. Based in Central London, Carole always carries a camera to record events.

You can connect with Carole via:

🌐 www.livingsuccess.co.uk

f facebook.com/carolerailtononline

in carolerailton frsa

🐦 @carolerailton

📷 @carole.railton